Informed Choice of Medical Services: Is the Law Just?

MARJ MILBURN

Ashgate

Aldershot • Burlington USA • Singapore • Sydney

Published by
Ashgate Publishing Ltd
Gower House
Croft Road
Aldershot
Hampshire GU11 3HR
England

Ashgate Publishing Company
131 Main Street
Burlington, VT 05401-5600 USA

Ashgate website: http://www.ashgate.com

British Library Cataloguing in Publication Data
Milburn, Marj
Informed choice of medical services : is the law just?
1. Medical care - Law and legislation 2. Feminist jurisprudence
I. Title
344.4'1'041

Library of Congress Control Number: 00-111407

ISBN 0 7546 1198 1

Printed and bound by Athenaeum Press, Ltd.,
Gateshead, Tyne & Wear.

Contents

Table of Cases

Preface

In this book I argue the case for external regulation of the medical community in order to protect the rights and safety of people receiving medical treatment. The evidence supporting this view is extensive and disturbing, particularly from the point of view of the person who suffers when their right to informed choice is violated. This is a major social problem in western societies and requires urgent resolution.

Acknowledgments

This work is dedicated to my mother, Shirley, who died during the preparation of the manuscript. Her belief in the relevance of this project to women's lives remains inspiring. Thank you to my sister, Zelda, for her encouragement and support, and to my friends and colleagues, particularly Beth Bennett and Marie West. Thank you to Paul McNeill and Loane Skene for taking valuable time to comment on early drafts of the first two chapters. This is deeply appreciated. Thank you also to my neighbour Jackie, who so generously made herself available at all times for discussions about 'work in progress'. Finally, thank you to Peter Singer, without whose encouragement I would not have begun this project.

Introduction

While much has been written in the past thirty years, particularly in the United States, about the moral right to informed choice of medical services changes to medical practice have been limited and medical authoritarianism, *as a culture*, remains deeply entrenched in western societies. Why is this still a problem? What is the solution? And what role should the law play in this solution?

In my view, medical authoritarianism, and its failure to recognise the right to informed choice, is a result of the traditional western philosophical, political, legal and scientific focus on rationality as *the* major influence on human behaviour. This ignores the central role of a person's values and beliefs in making decisions and choices. It also ignores the mass of historical evidence that power corrupts, breaking down the usual inhibitions that restrain the aggressive instincts inherent in human nature. The illusion that rationality dominates human affairs is therefore a dangerous one in that it fails to protect vulnerable members of a community from rights violations.

How extensive, then, is this problem? Relevant evidence spans more than a century, and demonstrates that women, as well as other disempowered groups, have been subjected to extensive violations of their right to informed choice, often with extremely serious consequences. Overall, the evidence is disturbing, profiling a major social problem requiring urgent resolution.

While the following discussion focuses on the exploitation of women by patriarchal medicine, this is not intended to discount the experiences of other groups whose right to self-determination is ignored by the medical community. Rather, it is intended to illustrate the claim that the abuse of power, masked by an over-confidence in the role of rationality in human behaviour, lies at the heart of the chronic problem of *un*informed choice. As women make up half of the human race, their oppression cannot be explained in terms of dominant groups versus minority groups. Rather, the hostility directed toward women is centred on perceived difference, which acts as a largely unconscious 'excuse' to indulge in the exercise of power over others who are, or who can be made, vulnerable.

Many other groups and individuals have also been discriminated against in this way by those who have the advantage of power. Indigenous Australians, while living in a wealthy country, suffer from a standard of 'health' equivalent to that of the most disadvantaged 'third world' nation. Medical practitioners have frequently treated, or refused to treat, these people in such a blatantly discriminatory manner that some groups have established their own health care services in an attempt to retain a sense of dignity. Health not only involves a person's physical state, but also their sense of identity and level of self-esteem. Shaming the entire Australian community, a recent court decision involving the 'stolen generation' of indigenous Australians considered a thumbprint on a 'consent' form acceptable evidence of a mother giving permission for her child to be taken from her by an all-powerful, white government. Again, 'difference' is used as an excuse to project internal hostilities onto a vulnerable Other.

Generally, this vulnerability of the Other is instinctively exploited wherever a power differential exists and there are no effective external constraints on the actions of the dominant party. This includes the client-practitioner encounter. Many medical practitioners still insist on controlling every aspect of this interaction, at the expense of client rights. The available evidence also indicates that the medical community often gives priority to the pursuit of its own interests, rather than those of the client. Even more disturbing is the apparent lack of insight into the unethical nature of denying the right to informed choice, as well as a lack of awareness that medical practitioners are fallible, just like everyone else. This is particularly dangerous given the group's power and prestige and the vulnerability of the ill person.

What, then, is the solution, and what role should the law play? The law in liberal democratic societies should protect vulnerable citizens from rights violations. However, common law jurisdictions in Australia, Canada, the United Kingdom and the United States have failed to fulfil this obligation in relation to informed choice. An examination of the relevant case law reveals a distinctly conservative judiciary. 'Justice' according to patriarchal legalism is not justice according to 'what is due' to health care clients *from their point of view*. A jurisprudence that acknowledges the central role of *power* in human affairs is urgently needed as a guideline for law reform that specifically aims at changing the balance of power within the clinical encounter. Only then will informed and voluntary choice of medical services be possible.

1 Informed Choice of Medical Services: Still a Problem?

Introduction

Atrocities committed by German medical scientists experimenting on concentration camp inmates and prisoners of war in the 1940s were the grim stimulus for the development of the concept of 'informed consent'.[1] However, evidence suggests that exposing people to possible harm without their knowledge remains endemic within the medical research community. Researchers claim that this is justified because it serves 'the greater good of society'. There is also evidence that placing people at risk without their consent is part of the culture of clinical medical practice, where practitioners take it upon themselves to weigh up the balance of risks and benefits on behalf of their clients 'for their own good'. Surprisingly, many medical practitioners sincerely believe that these human rights violations are justifiable. This lack of insight is dangerous. And it is particularly dangerous for the disempowered in societies where the privileges of class, wealth, education, patriarchy and power are jealously guarded.

In general, bioethicists have not confronted the problem of power abuse in medical research and clinical practice, despite the extensive literature on 'informed consent'.[2] Nor have they been prepared to acknowledge that informed and voluntary choice of medical services is a basic human right (Annas, 1998, pp.256-259). And yet, self-determination is the inalienable right of every human being.[3] Every person has the right to make their own life choices. This includes the right to make an informed choice about what is done, or not done, to their own body.

Nazi Germany and the Ethical Concept of 'Informed Consent'

Nazi medical scientists subjected concentration camp inmates and prisoners of war to horrific experimentation during the Second World War. The

Nuremberg Medical Trial, conducted by the allied forces at the end of the war, found 23 German medical scientists guilty of crimes against humanity. People were put into low pressure chambers so that the way in which they died could be 'scientifically' observed, others were exposed to freezing air and water, infected with typhus and malaria, sterilised and castrated, and murdered for anatomical specimens. Methods of producing rapid death were developed in order to exterminate 'unwanted groups'. The Nuremberg judges measured the culpability of the accused against a set of 10 principles, the most important being an absolute requirement for consent. This set of ethical principles became known as the *Nuremberg Code* (McNeill, 1993, pp.21-23).

And yet, German medical scientists were actively working on 'racial hygiene' practices well before the establishment of the Nazi Party. This included large scale sterilisation of 'unwanted' members of society. The Nazi exterminations were simply an extension of the mass killing of the mentally ill and retarded that took place in Germany prior to the war. Robert Proctor (1992) concludes that, given this background, it is hardly surprising that medical scientists exploited concentration camp inmates as subjects 'available' for human experimentation.[4] The Nazis did not force medical scientists to carry out these experiments. They were more than willing (pp.18-26).

Medical scientists also prospered under the Nazis. One of many was the Director of the Institute of Anatomy at Berlin University, Hermann Stieve, who studied the effect of awareness of impending execution on the menstrual cycle of women in concentration camps. At autopsy he established that the irregular bleeding suffered by these women was stress-induced.[5] Stieve published his results after the war as the leading German specialist in gynaecological anatomy at East Berlin's Humboldt University. Stieve, and many like him, were not indicted at Nuremberg (Pross, 1992, pp.37-38). In fact, several Nazi defendants from the Nuremberg Medical Trial were employed by the United States military after the war (Annas and Grodin, 1992, p.106).

Abuse of Research Subjects Beyond Nazi Germany

Abuses by medical scientists during the Second World War extended well beyond Nazi Germany. Similar atrocities were committed by Japanese researchers, although the United States agreed to give the Japanese immunity from prosecution in exchange for information about biological warfare. At least 15 of these Japanese medical scientists were subsequently appointed to senior positions in Japanese medical schools and research facilities. Many received high honours for their 'contribution to society'.

At the same time, medical research also became an extensive, well-funded project in the United States as a means to furthering the war effort. But, again, there was no concern for the welfare of research subjects. Prisoners and residents in mental asylums were deliberately infected with malaria, and then given experimental antidotes to test for efficacy and side effects. Consent was not considered necessary. Research subjects were seen as serving 'the greater good of society' (McNeill, pp.20-25).

Nor were the abuses of the Second World War an isolated aberration. Modern medicine developed in the hospitals of Eighteenth Century Paris as the result of experimentation on large numbers of impoverished people who provided a captured population of research subjects. Many studies involved infecting people with syphilis or gonorrhoea without their knowledge. There is also sufficient evidence to suggest that these practices continued throughout the Nineteenth Century[6] and into the early Twentieth Century (McNeill, pp.18-19).

Was the Nuremberg Code Effective?

The *Nuremberg Code* of 1946 was a pivotal statement of the ethical principles that ought to apply to research involving humans. As Jay Katz (1992) points out, the *Code* was remarkable in its uncompromising approach to absolute protection of the well-being of research subjects (p.226). Consent was the first and major principle of the *Code* and the only absolute principle of the new research ethics (Perley, Fluss, Bankowski and Simon, 1992, p.157).

However, George Annas (1992) claims that the *Code* has been largely ignored by the medical community (pp.204-205). According to Annas, the World Medical Association's *Declaration of Helsinki*, adopted by the World Medical Assembly in 1964, and the most frequently referred to ethical code, has always placed the researcher's choice and the interests of the research enterprise ahead of the well-being of research subjects (1998, p.251). David Rothman (1991) also claims that neither the horrors described at the Nuremberg trial, nor the ethical principles that emerged from it, had any significant impact on the medical research establishment in the United States (pp.70-77).

Disturbing Revelations

In 1966, Henry Beecher, a Harvard Professor of Anaesthetics, published an article in the *New England Journal of Medicine* pointing out that 22 research studies recently published in reputable medical journals were highly unethical. One of the constant problems with these studies was the lack of informed and voluntary consent. A year later, in 1967, M. H. Pappworth published a book entitled *Human Guinea Pigs,* which contained similar allegations of unethical research by British medical scientists (cited in McNeill, p.66).

One of the studies referred to in Beecher's article involved the Jewish Chronic Disease Hospital in New York. In this immunological study, which began in 1963, 22 frail and debilitated hospital residents were injected with live cancer cells without their knowledge. The principal investigator, Chester Southam, was a highly reputable medical scientist associated with a highly reputable academic institution. Southam stated at the subsequent inquiry that he simply did not wish to frighten patients by mentioning the word 'cancer', and insisted that he had done nothing wrong. Southam attempted to justify his actions by claiming that: 'An experimental relation has some elements of a therapeutic relationship ... The patients still think of you as a doctor, and I react to them as a doctor, and want to avoid frightening them unnecessarily'.

However, the Regents of the University of the State of New York, who were conducting the inquiry, disagreed, stating that the clinician, when acting as medical researcher, has no claim to the client-clinician relationship. The Regents concluded: 'No person can be said to have volunteered for an experiment unless he [*sic*] had first understood what he was volunteering for ... Deliberate non-disclosure of the material fact is no different from deliberate misrepresentation of such a fact' (Langer, 1992, p.147).

This raises the question as to whether informed and voluntary consent to participation in research is at all possible when the researcher is also clinician to the potential research subjects. Even if clinician-researchers are able to make a distinction between their clinical and research roles, it seems that Southam was right in claiming that patients 'still think of you as a doctor'. A study conducted in the United States in 1996 surveyed 1,900 outpatients in an attempt to determine their attitudes towards research. The results showed that a recommendation from a clinician to participate in research was interpreted by many as an endorsement of that project. People completely trusted their medical practitioner not to expose them to any harm (cited in Walton, 1998, pp.81-82).

Another study referred to by Beecher was carried out at the Willowbrook State School for intellectually disabled children from 1956 until 1970. This was an immunological experiment involving viral hepatitis. Children newly admitted to the institution were deliberately infected. The researchers, once again highly respected in their field, stated at a subsequent inquiry that they had obtained parental consent to involve the children in the research program. They also argued that the experimental work was justified by the potential benefits to society (Krugman and Giles, 1976). But, how could 'consent' be meaningful when the study was essentially unethical? And, exactly what information did the parents receive?

The Tuskegee Syphilis Study was another example of total disregard for the well-being of subjects. This 40 year project, carried out under the auspices of the Public Health Service, began in Alabama in the 1930s, with the aim of following the 'natural course' of syphilis. The subjects were 400 poor, black, male rural workers with the disease. The research project involved periodic blood tests and clinical examinations. Subjects were not told that they had syphilis and were not given the available treatment. However, they *were* told that the research procedures were special 'free treatments'. Results were periodically reported in the scientific literature without provoking any protests about the highly unethical nature of the project (Gillespie, 1989). Again, at no point did the researchers appear to develop any insight into the immorality of their activities (Jones, 1981).

Peer Review: Ethics Committees

As a result of these revelations, guidelines requiring ethics committee review of medical research involving humans were introduced in the United States and Canada in 1966, the United Kingdom in 1967, New Zealand in 1972 and Australia in 1973 (McNeill, p.66). Even so, there is ample evidence that people involved in medical research continue to be exposed to possible harm without their knowledge. It has been suggested that ethics committees have generally been ineffective in enforcing the requirements for informed and voluntary consent because they are 'captive' to their organisations, as well as the medical establishment. Nor are there any legal sanctions that would enable ethics committees to take action against offending researchers (Annas, 1998, pp.15-16).

More Disturbing Revelations

In 1970 a Federal Ethics Board in the United States held hearings related to in vitro fertilisation, concluding that there had been insufficient controlled animal experimentation to determine the long term effects of this procedure. Robyn Rowland points out that it is highly unlikely that the women involved in what was essentially experimentation were advised of this prior to giving their 'consent' to 'treatment' (cited in Scutt 1990, pp. 190-191).

In 1976 the United States Senate examined several unethical research studies, including one in which Mexican-American women were led to believe that they had been prescribed contraceptive pills, while they were actually subjects in an experiment testing the effectiveness of a new contraceptive. Some of these women were given a placebo, that is, no contraception at all. Again, researchers protested that the potential benefits to society outweighed the risks to individual subjects (McNeill, p.62).

In the early 1980s the Linda Loma Institutional Review Board in the United States gave approval for the implantation of a baboon's heart into the body of an infant with a fatal heart condition (McNeill, p.4). This was only one of many experimental organ transplants[7] that took place in the decades following Christaan Barnard's first heart transplant in 1967 (Walton, 1998, p.179). But, was consent obtained under such extreme duress really meaningful? And, were these researchers justified in even contemplating these procedures given the pain and suffering involved for the already desperately ill subject?

In 1986 a report entitled *American Nuclear Guinea Pigs: Three Decades of Radiation Experiments on United States Citizens* was published by the United States House of Representatives. Numerous studies had been carried out from the mid-1940s to the early 1970s by highly reputable medical scientists in highly reputable university departments throughout the country. Subjects, including hospital residents, prisoners and university students, did not know that they were being exposed to dangerous levels of radiation. The scientists involved prospered, publishing a number of scientific papers (cited in McNeill, pp.33-34).

In the late 1980s it was revealed that Herbert Green, a senior clinician at the National Women's Hospital in New Zealand, had begun recruiting women in the 1960s for participation in a research project aimed at observing whether or not cervical *carcinoma in situ* (cancer cells at a very early stage) would develop into invasive cancer. Instead of giving the women the standard treatment, Green simply observed their progress over a 20 year period. The women did not know that they were subjects in an experiment. A number of invasive cancers developed, and several women died. It is disturbing to read the detailed account of this 'unfortunate experiment' where Green, with a chilling lack of insight, insisted on continuing with the study even when it became clear to other medical personnel that women's lives were in danger (Coney and Bunkle, 1988).

Writing in 1994, Kenneth Rothman and Karin Michels claim that the unethical use of placebo controls is common in clinical trials testing new drug therapies for conditions such as rheumatoid arthritis, heart failure, hypertension and severe depression. These clinical trials involve assigning a placebo (no treatment) to a number of subjects. This provides a baseline against which to assess the effects of the experimental drug, which is given to the remaining study participants. Research subjects do not know whether they are receiving the experimental drug or the placebo. The problem is that all participants in the study are suffering from the condition being investigated, and yet, those given the placebo will not receive any treatment at all. Rothman and Michels claim that new drugs are tested against placebo, rather than the available 'best treatment', in order to save money, provide statistics that *seem* impressive, and place the drug on the market in the shortest possible time.

In December 1999 an Australian newspaper reported that: 'The first fatality linked to gene therapy ... has revitalised long-standing criticisms that cutting-edge experiments are proceeding too rapidly.' Jesse Gelsinger, aged 18, died after genetically engineered viruses were injected into his liver as part of a gene therapy experiment. The researchers were well aware of the serious risks involved in this experiment from their earlier work on monkeys. And yet, Jesse Gelsinger had not been informed of these risks.[8]

Katz (1992) believes that known abuses of research subjects are only the tip of the iceberg. Reflecting on his own 'countless discussions with research scientists', who openly admit that they 'tamper with consent' in order to obtain grants, get research projects started promptly, and further their own careers, Katz expresses concern that this is all done in the firm belief that consent is not important. The belief is that clinician-researchers can be trusted to protect subjects from harm. Katz goes on to point out how dangerous this assumption is, given the disturbing history of experimentation with humans and the known connection between the possession of power and the release of aggressive impulses (pp.231-237).

Does This Problem Extend to Medical Treatment?

Unfortunately, it does. Nor is there necessarily a clear dividing line between research and treatment. As is clear from the above discussion, new, or innovative, treatment strategies can still be at various stages of what is essentially an investigative process. In addition to the obvious examples, such as innovative organ transplants, there are less obvious ones, such as new drugs that are prematurely recommended as an improved treatment for a particular condition. This has significant implications for the issue of informed and voluntary choice, given that the necessary information that people need to make an informed decision may not even be available. As noted earlier, people tend to trust their medical practitioner to protect them from possible harm, regardless of whether this involves a research project or treatment. It is therefore the responsibility of the practitioner to be scrupulous about providing thorough and relevant information about proposed interventions, including their investigative status.

More Disturbing Revelations

In 1991, in Australia, the *New South Wales Royal Commission into Deep Sleep Therapy at Chelmsford Private Hospital*, where 24 people died as a direct result of medical treatment, found that the psychiatrists involved had acted without due care and that treatment was conducted without lawful or informed consent. These practitioners were treating people for depression by inducing prolonged narcosis, or drug-induced unconsciousness, a procedure which had been thoroughly condemned by their colleagues (Germove, 1993, pp.7-8).

Joan Lawrence, Past President of the Royal Australian and New Zealand College of Psychiatrists, writing in the *Medical Journal of Australia* in 1991, defined the central problem of the Chelmsford tragedy as '...psychiatrists with an absolute conviction of the rightness of their own beliefs...' indulging in '...the idiosyncratic use of power...' (pp.653-654).

A recent United States National Academy of Sciences report stated that more than 7,000 Americans die each year as a result of prescription errors.[9] While Merrilyn Walton (1998) acknowledges the difficulty that medical practitioners face in keeping up with the overwhelming flood of new drugs coming onto the market, she also points out that many also resist the introduction of constructive strategies for dealing with this problem, including the use of carefully researched clinical and practice guidelines (pp.109-110).

There is also a problem with standards of clinical competence in other areas. Walton notes that Australian medical practitioners are not required to participate in ongoing clinical education, and that Australia has made the least effort among comparable nations to deal with the problem of practitioner incompetence, with Canada and New Zealand being the most progressive. Again, the problem is compounded by the reluctance of many practitioners to admit to a lack of competence and a need for additional clinical training (pp.137-140). Clearly, this not only places clients at risk, but also means that they will be unaware that they are receiving less than competent medical care.

The 'Bristol Case' in the United Kingdom is a disturbing example of this. Stephen Bolsin, consultant cardiac anaesthetist at the Bristol Royal Infirmary in England, observed that two surgeon colleagues had two to three times the mortality rate of other centres in the United Kingdom for infants undergoing open-heart surgery. The problem was that the procedure was taking four hours rather than the standard one hour. This meant additional complications for the infants, leading to heart failure and death. All Bolsin's attempts to draw attention to this situation were ignored. It took six years of persistent complaints to hospital and government authorities before action was finally taken in 1996 (Walton, p.148). In a lecture given in Melbourne, Australia in November 1999, Bolsin stated that he considered the central problem to be one of power. During these six years one of the surgeons involved occupied an increasingly powerful position within the hospital community, and, Bolsin concludes, this made people particularly reluctant to act on complaints.[10]

Medical fraud and overservicing are also significant problems and have been well documented in both Australia and the United States (Walton, pp.37-40). Clearly, interventions carried out simply to make more money [11] unnecessarily expose people to the risks associated with those interventions (Moynihan, 1998, pp.9-10,35-38). Lou Opit, appointed Professor of Social and Preventive Medicine at Melbourne's Monash University in 1976, produced extensive evidence demonstrating that a great deal of the surgery being carried out in Australia at that time was unnecessary. Opit concluded that surgeons were taking advantage of what they saw as an opportunity to increase their incomes (cited in Rice, 1988, p.102).

Deborah Larned (1977) quotes Charles Lewis, Professor of Preventive Medicine at UCLA: 'Medicine is one of the few fields ... where, if your wife wants a new coat, all you have to do is a couple more hysterectomies and she can buy it' (pp.201-203). According to Ray Moynihan, unnecessary surgical interventions remain a significant problem at the turn of the century, particularly with regard to keyhole, or laparoscopic, surgery (pp.20,38). Clearly, informed consent, or refusal, is not going to occur in these circumstances.

The Exploitation of Women

Women in patriarchal societies are particularly vulnerable to exploitation by male medical practitioners. There was a major increase in the number of hysterectomies carried out in the United States in the 1960s and 1970s. By 1970 sterilisation by hysterectomy had become routine for women with normal pelvic function, as well as for those with relatively minor abnormalities. The decision to carry out these hysterectomies was made by the (male) medical practitioner.[12] Total hysterectomy was also carried out as a routine procedure after the completion of a woman's childbearing years. Male gynaecologists claimed that women did not need their uterus once they had completed their family (Larned, pp.198-200). And yet, no equivalent surgery has ever been proposed for men who have completed *their* families.

Clitoridectomy,[13] female circumcision[14] and female castration (removal of the ovaries) were performed extensively in France, Germany and the United States from the 1870s until the early 1950s. These procedures were carried out as 'treatment' for masturbation, mental illness and sexual desire. For nearly all of the 150,000 women in the United States who were surgically castrated there was a custodial male who gave permission for the surgery (Barker-Benfield, 1977, p.25).

While the prevalence of a 'custodial' male giving consent, instead of the woman concerned, constitutes a serious abuse of human rights, this situation is not surprising[15] given the patriarchal, and legally enforced, claim throughout most of human history that a woman is the property of her father, other male relative or husband (Scutt and Graham, 1984).

Lorne and Fay Rozovsky (1990) point out that Canadian common law has traditionally required a woman to obtain the consent of her spouse prior to sterilisation. It was not until 1986 that some Canadian jurisdictions passed legislation abolishing the requirement for spousal consent. But, despite these changes, the authors note that this practice continues even though it could be seen as contravening human rights legislation and the *Canadian Charter of Rights and Freedoms* (pp.30-31).

Nor are women informed when serious problems arise with existing treatments. In the mid-1970s officials of Dow Corning Corporation in the United States, and the medical community, were aware that Dow Corning's breast implants were leaking inside women's bodies. However, women were not advised of these problems and medical practitioners continued to carry out breast implantation on a wide scale. Phillipa Lowrey, of the Consumers' Health Forum of Australia, reports that many women complained to the Forum about not being adequately informed of the risks associated with this procedure. And when they raised this issue with their medical practitioners their experience was simply denied (cited in Scutt, 1997, p.302).

In 1991 a human hormone-based fertility drug, hPG, was linked to the deaths of two women in Australia. This drug had been administered to 1,500 women in Australia between 1964 and 1985, as well as to women in other countries, including the United States. But, while the cause of the problem was identified in 1985, and the use of the hormone stopped, women who had been treated with the drug were not informed that they were at risk. There were allegations of a 'cover-up' to protect those responsible. It was only after these concerns were raised in the Australian Parliament that government authorities contacted the women concerned to advise them of the situation (Scutt, pp.304-305).

Jocelynne Scutt concludes:

> A pattern may be discerned as identifying itself with monotonous regularity where women's health, medical treatment and 'informed consent' are concerned. The Dalkon Shield, diethylystylbestoral (DES), hPG and silicon implants are only examples of a much wider malaise. Women complain of discomfort, but the complaints are ignored or dismissed as hypochondria ... Doctors and manufacturers are alerted to the risks, or of manifold dangers. The product is withdrawn from the market. Women are still not told of the dangers... (p.306).

As Scutt points out, even if a woman is given an apparent 'choice', when adequate information is not provided, or the information provided is false or distorted, *there is no choice.* And, if significant risks are involved in proposed treatments is it ethical to even be offering a so-called 'choice'? (p.296). Nor is the widely used term 'informed consent' equivalent to 'informed choice'. 'Informed consent' implies that, when adequately informed, a person will automatically consent to whatever treatment options their medical practitioner proposes. However, this does not meet the ethical requirement for freedom of choice according to the principle of self-determination. Freedom of choice is the freedom to agree to, *or to refuse*, suggested treatment options.

Informed Choice of Medical Services and the Law

While a small number of court actions involving 'failure to inform' began to appear in English and Australian courts in the 1980s, a significant number of decided cases already existed in the United States (O'Sullivan, unpd, p.15), mainly as a result of the civil rights movement of the 1960s. Many people were no longer prepared to accept an authoritarian medical system which excluded them from the decision making processes involved in the management of their own health care (Darvall, 1993, pp.7-9).

From the Law of Battery to the Law of Negligence

Initially, people in the United States took action in the law of battery. However, there was a later shift to the law of negligence. The North American courts were concerned that the law of battery was a threat to the medical community because of the plaintiffs' relative ease of establishing the criteria for liability. The available alternative, the law of negligence, significantly reduced the chances of a plaintiff bringing a successful action. The ambiguity of the 'reasonable care' requirement, the ambiguity of standards of information disclosure, and the associated necessity of providing expert medical evidence, all placed a heavy burden on plaintiffs. So, too, did the need to establish the necessary causal link, both factual and legal, between the breach of duty and the damage suffered by the plaintiff.[16] The United States began allocating actions involving informed consent to the law of negligence in 1957, confirming the trend in 1960. Canada followed in 1980, and the United Kingdom a year later. Australia followed the Canadian and English precedents in 1983 in the South Australian Supreme Court and again in the High Court in 1992 (O'Sullivan, pp.16-27).

The Practitioner-Based Standard of Information Disclosure

Of all the jurisdictions under discussion, the United Kingdom has been the least progressive, consistently relying on the practitioner-based standard in 'failure to inform' cases. This standard defines adequate information disclosure in terms of the traditional practices of the medical community. However, those who argue for the right to informed choice have pointed out that this effectively gives those facing allegations of negligent practice the opportunity to decide, via their own colleagues, whether or not they have been negligent at law (Simanowitz, 1995, p.123).

In the United States in 1972, in *Canterbury v Spence*,[17] the judiciary appeared to take a progressive initiative. The court rejected the practitioner-based standard, stating that it was for the courts to determine the appropriate standard of disclosure, not the medical community. However, the majority of United States jurisdictions did not follow this precedent (Katz, 1977, pp.149-150). And, while Canada appeared to follow *Canterbury* in *Reibl v Hughes*[18] in 1980, apparently 'repudiating' the practitioner-based standard, a 1991 review of relevant cases in the 10 years following *Reibl* found that the great majority of these claims had not been successful. The courts consistently decided that, despite the apparent demise of the practitioner-based standard, any 'reasonable person' would follow their medical practitioner's advice (Robertson, 1991).

Again, in the 1992 landmark Australian case *Rogers v Whitaker*[19] the High Court appeared to reject the practitioner-based standard. But, while this decision seemed progressive, as Ian Dunn (1993) points out, Maree Whitaker may only have been successful because of her insistent pre-operative questioning as to any potential risks to her, then, remaining sight (p.352). If this were so, it would mean that the court had effectively relied on the practitioner-based standard after all, for this generally requires medical practitioners to respond to clients' questions.

This uncertainty remains unresolved following the outcome of the 1998 Australian High Court case, *Chappel v Hart*.[20] The High Court held that

Beryl Hart had expressed concern about the risk of damage to her vocal cords associated with recommended surgery, a risk which materialised and of which she had not been warned. Again, this conservative emphasis on 'question-asking' may unduly influence future court decisions.

Bioethics: Is Trust Enough?

Allen Buchanan and Dan Brock (1990) claim that, with regard to informed choice, 'this battle has been largely won' for the mentally competent adult seeking medical care (p.2). Given the evidence referred to above, this claim is obviously not sustainable. Nevertheless, such optimism is typical of the bioethical literature, where the assumption that medical practitioners generally act beneficently dominates discussions of the ideal client-practitioner relationship (Pellegrino and Thomasma, 1988; Brock, 1991).

While discussions of ideal models of the clinical encounter are important, bioethicists almost completely ignore the problem of the power differential between client and practitioner and the implications of this for the vulnerable party. Even the few bioethicists who *do* acknowledge this power differential, and the potential for abuse, still see the solution as trust in the benevolence of the practitioner. But, as Sheila McLean (1999) puts it: 'It is unacceptable in liberal democracies that power can be exercised free of any constraints and free of accountability. Therefore, society must establish mechanisms which ensure external scrutiny of the medical enterprise, as well as individual practitioners' (p.15).

Speaking to *The Australian* newspaper in December 1997, Liz Swinburne, a teacher, told of her continuing anger about the way she was informed of a positive diagnosis of breast cancer five years earlier. On ringing her medical practitioner, as instructed, to find out the results of her mammogram, Ms Swinburne was advised of her diagnosis, and that she had been booked for surgery, by the *receptionist*. 'I just fell to pieces. I was sitting in a room alone, with a classroom of girls waiting for me.' In the same article, Rob Simons, Professional Education and Training Manager with The Anti-Cancer Council of Victoria, claimed that medical practitioners are still not prepared to provide the information that people want and need.[21]

In December 1999, Giovanna Scarpa spoke to *The Weekend Australian:*

> Four years after nearly joining the 18,000 Australians a year estimated to die from adverse medical events in hospital, Giovanna Scarpa is still angry and hurt by the "cruelty" of her situation. Mrs Scarpa, now 54, says she is upset not just at the pain she still endures after her heart was punctured by exploratory wires during a test in a Melbourne hospital, but because the specialist involved did

not return her calls. "... I rang him three times to tell him how sick I was and he never returned my phone calls. It's so cruel. Why didn't he want to know me anymore?" [22]

Clearly, trust is not enough.

Notes

1 I am particularly indebted to the work of George Annas and Paul McNeill, which provided essential material for this chapter.

2 While a number of bioethicists did advocate a weak version of 'rights talk' in the 1960s and 1970s, they did not address the central role of power in the client-practitioner encounter, and in the 1980s there was an almost total retreat from 'rights talk' of any kind.

3 While there are differing views, and an extensive literature, on the nature of autonomy, or self-determination, Beauchamp and Childress (1994) refer to it as the *rule of self*, free from coercion and personal limitations that inhibit the making of choices meaningful to that individual (pp.121-126). The modern concept of autonomy has been deeply influenced by the Eighteenth Century German philosopher Immanuel Kant (1990) who argued that respect for autonomy is based on each individual's inherent value as a human being, and that it is therefore wrong for a person to be used as a means to someone else's ends.

4 Proctor points out that German racial theorists learned much from the Americans. By the late 1920s at least 15,000 people incarcerated in prisons and mental institutions in the United States had been sterilised (p.21).

5 In 1989 Richard Toellner, medical historian, claimed that: '...a medical profession, who accepts mass murder of sick people as a normality, and to a large degree explicitly approves of it as a necessary, justified act for the sake of the community, has failed and betrayed its mission' (cited in Pross, 1992, p.45). Pross concludes: 'The system of silence, lies, half-truths, excuses, and angry denials of the last four decades is in retreat. The open debate about the Nazi past has raised the consciousness of many German doctors and of parts of the German public toward contemporary medical abuses. It has shaken the German doctors' self-image of infallibility, of a profession that stands above political and social forces and that presumably has always had a clean shirt and has acted out of noble, altruistic motives' (p.47).

6 Katz (1992) notes that in 1892 a Swedish researcher 'used' young children as subjects in vaccine experiments. The researcher stated that he would have 'used' animals but these were too difficult to obtain and too expensive to keep (p.230). In 1904 Colonel Strong, later Professor of Tropical Medicine at Harvard University, vaccinated condemned criminals in Manila with live plague bacteria without their consent. Richard Gillespie (1989) gives an account of similar experiments conducted under coercive institutional control (p.9). In Nineteenth Century North America medical practitioners put slaves into pit ovens to study the effects of heat stroke, poured scalding water over them as an experimental treatment for typhoid fever, and 'used' them to experiment with internal surgery (McNeill, p.19).

7 The recipient of the first human heart transplant died shortly after the surgery was carried out. Nevertheless, another 118 people subsequently underwent this procedure. Most of them died. It was decades before the success rate improved (Walton, 1998, p.179).

8 *The Sunday Age,* 5 December 1999.

9 *The Australian,* 2 December 1999.

10 Stephen Bolsin, *The Bristol Case,* public lecture, Alfred Hospital, 17 November 1999. According to Walton (1998), the United States comes closest to protecting the public in this regard, with a central register of incidents indicating a lack of clinical competence. This information is available to medical boards, although not to consumer groups. It should also be noted that the primary goal of this government initiative was to contain the costs of medical negligence litigation (pp.152-153).

11 See also Wilson, Chappell and Lincoln (1986). These authors demonstrate that while this problem has received little public attention in Canada, nevertheless, it does exist.

12 Many gynaecologists also advised that hysterectomy was therapeutically indicated as a means of preventing the potential development of uterine cancer. However, they failed to tell women that the death rate for hysterectomy was 1,000 out of every million women annually, and was, in fact, higher than the death rate from uterine/cervical cancer (Larned, 1977, pp.198-200).

13 Surgical removal of the clitoris.

14 Surgical removal of the hood of the clitoris.

15 For example, in Eighteenth Century England William Blackstone and other 'eminent' jurists codified laws that defined women as *femmes covertes*, that is, 'hidden' within the husband or male relative's domestic 'realm'. At law, women had no individual identity. The law sanctioned the sale of daughters and wives as 'property'. Any property a woman brought to a marriage, or any earnings made during the marriage, were automatically the property of the husband (Scutt and Graham, 1984, pp.87-91). Throughout medieval Europe the law sanctioned the murder of an adulterous wife by her husband, in addition to his legal right to inflict corporal punishment as he wished (O'Faolain and Martines, 1979, pp.188ff).

16 Since consent clearly involves an information component it was initially accepted by some courts that a failure to provide certain significant information pre-operatively could invalidate an apparent consent and leave a surgeon liable for battery, even though the procedure had been carried out with due care. Since the very act of carrying out the procedure without valid consent constituted the legal wrong, that is, unlawful touching, the plaintiff found it easier to prove causation. There were also other advantages to an action in battery not available to plaintiffs suing in negligence (O'Sullivan, unpd, pp.16ff).

17 464 F 2d 772 (1972) (US Ct of Apps, DC Cir).

18 (1980) 114 DLR (3d) 1 (Can SC), 2 SCR 880.

19 (1992) 175 CLR 479; 109 ALR 625 (HCA).

20 [1998] HCA 55.

21 *The Weekend Australian,* 20-21 December 1997.

22 *The Weekend Australian,* 11-12 December 1999.

References

Annas, G. J. (1992), 'The Nuremberg Code in US Courts: Ethics versus Expediency', in G. J. Annas and M. A. Grodin (eds), *The Nazi Doctors and the Nuremberg Code: Human Rights in Human Experimentation*, New York: Oxford University Press, pp. 201-222.

Annas, G. J. (1998), *Some Choice: Law, Medicine, and the Market*, New York: Oxford University Press.

Annas, G. J. and Grodin, M. A. (1992), 'Judgment and Aftermath', in G. J. Annas and M. A. Grodin (eds), *The Nazi Doctors and the Nuremberg Code: Human Rights in Human Experimentation*, New York: Oxford University Press, pp. 94-107.

Barker-Benfield, G. J. (1977), 'Sexual Surgery in Late Nineteenth Century America', in C. Dreifus (ed), *Seizing our Bodies: The Politics of Women's Health*, New York: Vintage Books, pp. 13-41.

Beauchamp, T. L. and Childress, J. F. (1994), *Principles of Biomedical Ethics*, (4th ed), New York: Oxford University Press.

Beecher, H. (1966), 'Ethics and Clinical Research', *New England Journal of Medicine*, vol. 274, pp. 1354-1360.

Brock, D. W. (1991), 'The Ideal of Shared Decision-Making Between Physicians and Patients', *Kennedy Institute of Ethics Journal*, March, pp. 28-47.

Brody, H. (1992), *The Healer's Power*, New Haven: Yale University Press.

Buchanan, A. E. and Brock, D. W. (1990), *Deciding for Others: The Ethics of Surrogate Decision-Making*, Cambridge: Cambridge University Press.

Coney, S. and Bunkle, P. (1988), 'An Unfortunate Experiment', *Bioethics News*, vol. 8 (1), pp. 3-31.

Darvall, L. (1993), *Law and Social Change: The Impact of Bioethics, Feminism and Rights Movements on Medical Decision-Making*, Sydney: Dartmouth.

Dunn, I. (1993), 'What should doctor tell you?' *Law Institute Journal*, April, pp. 268-271.

Germove, J. (1993), *Getting Away with Murder: Medical Negligence, Informed Consent and Access to Justice*, Department of Social Health Studies, University of Newcastle, New South Wales.

Gillespie, R. (1989), 'Research on Human Subjects: An Historical Overview', *Bioethics News*, January, pp. 4-15.

Jones, J. H. (1981), *Bad Blood: The Tuskegee Syphilis Experiment*, New York: Free Press.

Kant, I. (1990), *Foundations of the Metaphysics of Morals and What is Enlightenment?* (2nd ed), Beck, L. W. (trans), New York: Macmillan. First published 1784, 1785.

Katz, J. (1977), 'Informed Consent – A Fairy Tale? Law's Vision', *University of Pittsburgh Law Review*, vol. 39 (2), pp. 137-174.

Katz, J. (1992), 'The Consent Principle of the Nuremberg Code: Its Significance Then and Now', in G. J. Annas and M. A. Grodin (eds), *The Nazi Doctors and the Nuremberg Code: Human Rights in Human Experimentation*, New York: Oxford University Press, pp. 227-239.

Krugman, S. and Giles, J. P. (1976), 'Viral Hepatitis: New Light on an Old Disease', in S. Gorovitz, et al., (eds), *Moral Problems in Medicine*, Englewood Cliffs, New Jersey: Prentice-Hall, pp. 123-125.

Langer, E. (1976), 'Human Experimentation: New York Verdict Affirms Patient's Rights', in S. Gorovitz, et al., (eds), *Moral Problems in Medicine*, Englewood Cliffs, New Jersey: Prentice-Hall, pp. 142-150.

Larned, D. (1977), 'The Epidemic in Unnecessary Hysterectomy', in C. Dreifus (ed), *Seizing our Bodies: The Politics of Women's Health*, New York: Vintage Books, pp. 195-208.

Lawrence, J. (1991), 'Inquiries into Psychiatry: Chelmsford and Townsville', *Medical Journal of Australia*, vol. 155, pp. 652-654.

McLean, S. A. M. (1999), *Old Law, New Medicine: Medical Ethics and Human Rights*, London and New York: Rivers Oram Publishers.

McNeill, P. M. (1993), *The Ethics and Politics of Human Experimentation*, Cambridge, New York and Melbourne: Cambridge University Press.

Moynihan, R. (1998), *Too Much Medicine*, Sydney: ABC Books.

O'Faolain, J. and Martines, L. (eds), (1979), *Not in God's Image: Women in History*, London: Virago.

O'Sullivan, J. (unpd), *The Professional Versus the Material Risks Standards of Risk Disclosure: The Appropriate Standard for Australia*, Master of Laws Thesis (1988), Monash University, Melbourne.

Pellegrino, E. D. and Thomasma, D. C. (1988), *For the Patient's Good: The Restoration of Beneficence in Health Care*, New York: Oxford University Press.

Perley, S. Fluss, S. Bankowski, Z. and Simon, F. (1992), 'The Nuremberg Code: An International Overview', in G. J. Annas and M. A. Grodin (eds), *The Nazi Doctors and the Nuremberg Code: Human Rights in Human Experimentation*, New York: Oxford University Press, pp. 149-173.

Proctor, R. N. (1992), 'Nazi Doctors, Racial Medicine, and Human Experimentation', in G. J. Annas and M. A. Grodin (eds), *The Nazi Doctors and the Nuremberg Code: Human Rights in Human Experimentation*, New York: Oxford University Press, pp. 17-31.

Pross, C. (1992), 'Nazi Doctors, German Medicine, and Historical Truth', in G. J. Annas and M. A. Grodin (eds), *The Nazi Doctors and the Nuremberg Code: Human Rights in Human Experimentation*, New York: Oxford University Press, pp. 32-52.

Rice, S. (1988), *Some Doctors Make You Sick*, North Ryde, New South Wales: Angus & Robertson.

Robertson, G. (1991), 'Informed Consent Ten Years Later: The Impact of Reibl v Hughes', *The Canadian Bar Review*, vol. 70 (3), pp. 423-447.

Rothman, D. (1991), *Strangers at the Bedside: A History of How Law and Bioethics Transformed Medical Decision Making*, New York: Basic Books.

Rothman, K. J. and Michels, K. B. (1994), 'The Continuing Unethical Use of Placebo Controls', *New England Journal of Medicine*, August, pp. 394-398.

Rozovsky, L. and Rozovsky, F. (1990), *The Canadian Law of Consent to Treatment*, Toronto and Vancouver: Butterworths.

Scutt, J. A. (1990), *Women and the Law: Commentary and Materials*, North Ryde, New South Wales: Law Book Company.

Scutt, J. A. (1997), *The Incredible Woman: Power & Sexual Politics*, *Volume 1*, Melbourne: Artemis Publishing.

Scutt, J. A. and Graham, D. (1984), *For Richer, For Poorer: Money, Marriage and Property Rights*, Melbourne: Penguin Books.

Simanowitz, A. (1995), 'Law Reform and Medical Negligence Litigation: The UK Position', in S. A. M. McLean (ed), *Law Reform and Medical Injury Litigation*, Aldershot: Dartmouth, pp. 119-146.

The Nuremberg Code, (1946), in *Trials of War Criminals before the Nuremberg Military Tribunals under Control Council Law No. 10*, vol. 2, 1949, Washington, D.C: United States Government Printing Office, pp. 181-182.

Walton, M. (1998), *The Trouble with Medicine: Preserving the Trust Between Patients and Doctors*, St Leonards, New South Wales: Allen & Unwin.

Wilson, P. R. Chappell, D. and Lincoln, R. (1986), 'Policing Physician Abuse in British Columbia: An Analysis of Current Policies', *Canadian Public Policy*, vol. 12 (1), pp. 236-244.

Cases

Canterbury v Spence 464 F 2d 772 (1972) (US Ct of Apps, DC Cir).
Chappel v Hart [1998] HCA 55.
Reibl v Hughes (1980) 114 DLR (3d) 1 (Can SC), 2 SCR 880.
Rogers v Whitaker (1992) 175 CLR 479; 109 ALR 625 (HCA).

2 Informed Choice: Legal Doctrine or Ethical Concept?

Introduction

The North American common law doctrine of 'informed consent'[1] and the Anglo-Australian 'duty of disclosure' have been criticised by bioethicists for focussing too narrowly on the required standard of information disclosure. The concern is that this does not address the complexities of client-practitioner communication. Bioethicists have also pointed out that the courts appear unable to resolve a persistent conflict between the principles of client choice and practitioner duty. This conflict was evident in 1957 in *Salgo v Leland Stanford Jr University Board of Trustees*,[2] the first case in which the term 'informed consent' was used. Justice Bray found that the defendant had the duty to disclose those facts necessary for the client to give an intelligent consent to proposed treatment. And yet, he also made the highly ambiguous statement that: '…in discussing the element of risk a certain amount of discretion must be employed consistent with the full disclosure of facts necessary to an informed consent' (at 181).

That this conflict remains unresolved is obvious from the outcome of the 1993 case *Arato v Avedon*,[3] in which the California Supreme Court ruled that the defendants were not required to have advised their client, Miklos Arato, that his illness was terminal, despite the fact that he had made it clear that he would want to be informed of this. George Annas (1998) notes that the court acknowledged the continued 'critical standoff' between client choice and practitioner 'paternalism', while at the same time perpetuating the problem by focussing on a narrow question related to disclosure (pp.59-60).

'Informed Consent' as Legal Doctrine: The United States and Canada

The legal doctrine of 'informed consent' originated, as already noted, in the United States. While there were several medical malpractice cases that also involved consent in the late Nineteenth and early Twentieth Centuries (Seabourne, 1995), the volume of cases did not expand significantly until the early 1970s (Wadlington, 1995). Canada experienced an increase in the mid-1980s (Benidickson, 1995), the United Kingdom in the early 1980s (Simanowitz, 1995) and Australia in the 1990s.

While the legal duty of medical practitioners to disclose information about the known risks, and other aspects, of proposed treatment is often referred to by the North American term 'informed consent', this term is not part of Anglo-Australian law, which uses the phrase 'duty of disclosure'.[4] It should also be noted that while many jurisdictions have introduced a variety of statutory measures related to 'informed consent' and the 'duty to disclose' the major developments have occurred within the common law.

'Informed Consent' and the Law of Battery

Initially, as noted in the previous chapter, actions involving allegations of failure to inform were brought in the law of trespass, or battery, which involves the intentional interference with the body of another person without their consent (Rozovsky and Rozovsky, 1990, pp.116-117). As consent clearly involves an information component, some courts accepted the argument that failure to provide certain significant information pre-operatively could invalidate an apparent consent and leave the surgeon liable for battery, regardless of the fact that the procedure had been carried out with due care.[5] Examples of battery in the medical context include: carrying out a tubal ligation, without consent, while performing a caesarean section; administering a spinal anaesthetic when permission had specifically been given for a general anaesthetic; administering a blood transfusion against the person's wishes; and sexual battery associated with medical treatment (Bennett, 1997, pp.53-54).

However, despite the relative ease of establishing the criteria for liability, actions brought in battery were not always successful. The much quoted 1914 case *Schloendorff v Society of New York Hospital*[6] did not secure a verdict for the plaintiff despite the statement by Justice Cardozo that: 'Every human being of adult years and sound mind has a right to determine what should be done with his [*sic*] own body; and a surgeon who performs an operation without his patient's consent commits an assault, for which he is liable in damages' (at 93). The defendant medical practitioner had removed a fibroid tumour after the client had consented to an abdominal examination under anaesthesia, specifically requesting that no surgery be carried out. However, the court did not find a violation of 'informed consent', nor make any comments about what information a person needs in order to exercise the right to determine what should be done to their own body.

In *Regina v Bolduc and Bird*, [7] in Canada, in 1967, the court's decision also went against the plaintiff. The defendant medical practitioner allowed a friend, who was not medically trained, to watch while he carried out a vaginal examination. A prosecution for indecent assault followed. The issue for the court was whether the plaintiff's consent covered the entire act. That is, was the fact that Bird was not a medical practitioner essential to the nature of the act, or was it merely collateral?

The court held that it was merely collateral and that, therefore, the plaintiff had consented to the examination with that person present. This Supreme Court decision reversed that of the British Columbia Court of Appeal, which had held that consent *was* legally invalidated because the plaintiff had only consented to being examined in the presence of medically qualified people. As Bird was not medically qualified his presence amounted to a drastic change in the essential nature of the act to which the plaintiff had consented (Somerville, 1981, p.745).

The Move to the Law of Negligence

Nevertheless, despite difficulties for some plaintiffs bringing actions in the law of battery, as discussed in the previous chapter, the North American courts became concerned that the relative ease of establishing the criteria for liability was a threat to the medical community. The judiciary was also concerned about the exposure of medical practitioners to the social stigma associated with actions brought in battery. As a result, the courts initiated a shift to the law of negligence (O'Sullivan, unpd, pp.19-20). The two United States cases that were particularly important in the move from battery to negligence were *Salgo v Leland Stanford Jr University Board of Trustees* in 1957 and *Natanson v Kline*[8] in 1960. Of the two cases, *Natanson* gave the clearest explanation of the reasons for this change (O'Sullivan, p.21).

The common law tort (civil wrong) of negligence provides for monetary compensation for injuries suffered as a result of negligent statements, acts or omissions. In order to make a successful claim, a plaintiff must be able to prove that the defendant owed them a duty of care, that they breached that duty by failing to provide the necessary level of care, and that the plaintiff suffered damage as a result. In order to establish that the defendant owed the plaintiff a duty of care, the plaintiff must demonstrate foreseeability of the risk, as well as proximity between the plaintiff and the defendant (Bennett, pp.43-44). Negligence law is therefore defined in terms of a responsibility, or duty of care, not to injure another person, rather than in terms of a right not to be injured (Darvall, 1993, p.29).

As noted earlier, plaintiffs now faced major obstacles to establishing the criteria for liability. This was largely the result of the ambiguities involved in the 'reasonable care' requirement, in the standards of information disclosure, and in the requirement to establish the causal link, both factual and legal, between the breach of duty and the damage suffered (O'Sullivan, p.17). Given that the required standard of disclosure used by the courts has generally been the practitioner-based standard, most plaintiffs have failed at this point.

Those few who have managed to clear this first obstacle have generally failed in their attempt to 'prove' causation, the second major obstacle. Causation will not be established if the plaintiff's injuries could have been caused by something other than the alleged breach of duty, or if the plaintiff's injuries would have occurred regardless of the alleged breach. The plaintiff must prove that they would not have undergone the treatment if they had been warned of the risks (Bennett, p.51). As the only proof that plaintiffs can offer is their word that they would not have undergone the proposed treatment if they had been warned of the risks, and as the courts have frequently concluded that the plaintiff's word is not 'reliable', there is little chance of success. The law of negligence also generally requires plaintiffs to provide expert medical evidence. This has proven particularly difficult, given that few medical practitioners are willing to testify against their colleagues (Freckelton, 1999a).

Standards of Disclosure

According to the practitioner-based standard of information disclosure, the defendant medical practitioner is not liable if expert witnesses state that the practitioner's action was an accepted practice within the medical community at the time of the alleged incident. Clearly, this has usually been relatively easy for the defendant to establish via sympathetic colleagues. And, as already noted, while it seemed that the practitioner-based standard had been rejected in the United States in 1972, in *Canterbury v Spence*,[9] where the court took on the responsibility for determining the appropriate standard of disclosure, this precedent was not followed by other United States jurisdictions. In *Canterbury,* a young man had sought medical advice about the management of back problems and was advised that a laminectomy was the appropriate treatment, to which he agreed. However, he was not informed that this surgical procedure involved a 1 per cent risk of paralysis, a risk that materialised post-operatively. The Court of Appeals of the District of Columbia decided that: '...respect for the patient's right of self-determination on particular therapy demands a standard set by law for physicians rather than one which physicians may or may not impose upon themselves' (at 784).

Therefore, the standard applied to the duty of disclosure should be the 'reasonable person' standard: '...conduct which is reasonable under the circumstances' (at 785). The court also stated that a risk is 'material', and therefore must be disclosed, '...when a reasonable person, in what the physician knows or should know to be the patient's position, would be likely to attach significance to the risk or cluster of risks in deciding whether or not to forego the proposed therapy' (at 787). The scope of required disclosure was to be assessed according to the client's needs.[10]

However, Jay Katz (1977) believes that *Canterbury* was not as progressive as it seemed in that the court continued to allow medical practitioners to exercise discretion with regard to disclosure by means of the *therapeutic privilege*. Practitioners could claim *therapeutic privilege* if they considered that withholding information was essential to the client's well-being, effectively invoking the practitioner-based standard (p.158). Katz' observation seems particularly astute given the outcome in *Arato v Avedon,* 21 years after *Canterbury*, where, despite the court's reference to the doctrine of 'informed consent', Miklos Arato's wish to be told the truth about his illness and prognosis was found to be irrelevant. The court permitted the defendants to call expert medical witnesses who testified that it was not standard practice in the medical community in 1980 to disclose specific life expectancy data to clients. The court subsequently held that the defendants would not have been required to make this disclosure as part of the accepted medical standard of care at that time (cited in Annas, 1998, pp.56-60).

Nevertheless, in the 1980 Canadian case *Reibl v Hughes*,[11] the practitioner-based standard was once more 'repudiated'. The plaintiff in *Reibl* had suffered paralysis following surgery to clear a narrowed carotid artery. He claimed that he had not been informed of this known risk, and that he would not have undergone the surgery, which was not urgent, if he had been informed. He also argued that he would have based his decision on the fact that he was only 18 months away from qualifying for a retirement pension. Following the surgery, and the materialisation of the risk, he was no longer able to work and, therefore, could not qualify for the pension. The plaintiff was successful.

And yet, as noted earlier, Gerald Robertson (1991), in a review of cases involving informed consent in the 10 years following *Reibl*, concluded that, despite the apparent doctrinal advances in that case, the Canadian courts have continued to effectively rely on a practitioner-based standard by holding that any 'reasonable' person would follow their medical practitioner's instructions. In 82 per cent of the 117 cases analysed by

Robertson, the informed consent claim was dismissed. In 45 of these cases the defendant was held to have been negligent in failing to disclose material information, but in 56 per cent of these 45 cases the plaintiff failed to satisfy the test for causation. Robertson concludes that while the courts assume that 'reasonable' people trust their medical practitioner and are therefore likely to agree to proposed treatment, even if associated risks are disclosed:

> ... these assumptions seem inconsistent with the policy reasons which led the Supreme Court of Canada in *Reibl* to reject the professional standards test as the basis for determining how much information patients ought to receive (p.434).

The Legal 'Duty of Disclosure': Australia and the United Kingdom

In comparison to North America, there have been relatively few cases involving 'failure to warn' in both Australia and the United Kingdom. The first significant English case was *Bolam v Friern Hospital Management Committee*[12] in 1957. Although this was the same year that Justice Cardozo introduced the term 'informed consent' in *Salgo*, O'Sullivan notes that it is unlikely that the English judiciary were aware of the new American legal doctrine (p.80). The plaintiff in *Bolam* was advised to undergo a course of Electro Convulsive Treatment, but was not advised of the known risk of fractures. He subsequently suffered a fractured pelvis. The plaintiff alleged negligence in that the defendant medical practitioner had not administered an anaesthetic, or muscle relaxants, prior to treatment, and failed to have him restrained during the procedure. The plaintiff also alleged 'failure to warn'. He was not successful. Justice McNair accepted expert medical evidence that the defendant medical practitioner had not 'fallen below a standard of practice recognized as proper by a competent reasonable body of opinion' (at 587). McNair's formulation of the practitioner-based standard of information disclosure is often referred to as the *Bolam* test.

The next English case involving 'failure to warn', *Chatterton v Gerson*,[13] did not occur until 1981. But, although the English judiciary were now aware of the North American legal doctrine of 'informed consent', they did not question the relevance of the *Bolam* test to 'information disclosure', although they did follow the North American move to allocating 'failure to warn' cases to negligence. The *Bolam* test was also endorsed by the House of Lords in 1985 in *Sidaway v Board of Governors of Bethlem Royal Hospital and Others*,[14] despite a query being raised as to the relevance of this standard to medical malpractice cases involving 'failure to warn'.

The first two Australian cases involving information disclosure, *Hart v Herron*,[15] and *D v S*,[16] went to battery. *Hart v Herron* involved a claim by the plaintiff that he had been treated with 'deep sleep therapy' at Chelmsford Private Hospital without his consent. The plaintiff was awarded damages against the defendant medical practitioner for wrongful imprisonment, assault and negligence. In *D v S* the plaintiff alleged negligent performance of a mammoplasty, as well as failure to inform that significant scarring might occur. Justice Matheson found that the plaintiff had been assaulted (Tan, 1987).

However, Australian courts followed *Chatterton v Gerson* and *Reibl v Hughes* in allocating 'failure to warn' to negligence in the 1983 South Australian Supreme Court case *F v R* [17] (O'Sullivan, pp.26-27). This ruling was endorsed by the High Court of Australia in 1992 in *Rogers v Whitaker*.[18] Following the move to negligence, plaintiffs were generally unsuccessful in failure to inform cases[19] until the 1992 landmark case of *Rogers v Whitaker*, which rejected the practitioner-based standard of disclosure.

Standards of Disclosure and the Australian Courts

In *F v R*, the leading Australian case prior to *Rogers v Whitaker*, the plaintiff, pregnant with her third child, and not wishing to have more children, consulted a gynaecologist for advice on methods of sterilisation. The medical practitioner recommended a tubal ligation, but did not inform the plaintiff that there was a failure rate of between 0.5 to 1 per cent. Following the tubal ligation, the plaintiff became pregnant. Chief Justice King, of the South Australian Supreme Court, observed that the defendant medical practitioner would have been under a duty to disclose this information if the plaintiff had specifically asked about the possibility of a subsequent pregnancy.

King also noted that it would be better medical practice, as well as consistent with the rights and interests of clients, to warn of this risk associated with tubal ligation. King stated: 'It is my opinion that … the duty extends, not only to the disclosure of real risks of misfortune inherent in the treatment, but also any real risk that the treatment, especially if it involves major surgery, may prove ineffective' (at 191).

And yet, King then went on to conclude that, because this instance of failure to disclose was in accordance with current medical practice, the defendant had not been negligent in her 'failure to warn' (at 191). This is the same Chief Justice King who, in the same case, rejected the practitioner-based standard of information disclosure:

> The ultimate question ... is not whether the defendant's conduct accords with the practices of his [*sic*] profession or some part of it, but whether it conforms to the standard of reasonable care demanded by the law. That is a question for the court and the duty of deciding it cannot be delegated to any profession or group in the community' (at 194).

It seems remarkable that, given all the reasons put forward by Chief Justice King for supporting the plaintiff's right to know about the risk of failure involved in a tubal ligation, he should then reach a decision which denied that right, but was in accordance with current medical practice.

Nevertheless, in *Rogers v Whitaker*, in the High Court of Australia in 1992, Maree Whitaker successfully sued an ophthalmic surgeon for carrying out treatment that resulted in almost total blindness. He had not warned her of the known risk of sympathetic ophthalmia, the risk that any damage to the eye involved in the surgery could extend to the other eye. The High Court held that the surgeon's failure to warn of this risk constituted negligence, rejecting the practitioner-based standard of disclosure (Skene, 1993):

> ...a risk is material if, in the circumstances of the particular case, a reasonable person in the patient's position, if warned of the risk, would be likely to attach significance to it or if the medical practitioner is or should reasonably be aware that the particular patient, if warned of the risk, would be likely to attach significance to it (at 490).

Factors that now had to be taken into account with regard to disclosing risks of a proposed procedure included the nature of the matter to be disclosed, the nature of the treatment, and the desire of the particular client for information, as well as the client's general circumstances (Malcolm, 1994). Nevertheless, the duty to disclose was once again qualified by the *therapeutic privilege*.

And yet, as noted in the previous chapter, while *Rogers v Whitaker* has generally been considered progressive, Ian Dunn (1993) points out that Maree Whitaker may only have been successful because of her insistent pre-operative questioning of the surgeon as to any potential risks to her then remaining sight. If Maree Whitaker had not expressed this concern the court's decision may very well have been different. It can therefore be argued that the court's obvious reliance on the plaintiff's 'question-asking' did not *actually test* any of the new doctrinal requirements for information disclosure. 'Question-asking' is an integral part of the practitioner-based standard, which 'allows' that a medical practitioner must truthfully answer a client's questions, unless the practitioner is invoking the *therapeutic privilege*.

This view is supported by the ambiguity of Justice Gaudron's statement about the 'question-asking' issue:

> Even if a court were satisfied that a reasonable person in the patient's position would be unlikely to attach significance to a particular risk, the fact that the patient asked questions revealing concern about the risk would make the doctor aware that this patient did in fact attach significance to the risk. Subject to the therapeutic privilege, the question would therefore require a truthful answer (at 487).

Therefore, with the broader requirements of information disclosure referred to in *Rogers v Whitaker* untested, as well as the continued allowance of the *therapeutic privilege,* it could be argued that despite the apparent doctrinal advances of this judgment, future plaintiffs remained vulnerable to conservative interpretations of the procedural requirements in negligence.

The comments of the Australian High Court in *Breen v Williams,*[20] in 1996, also raise a doubt as to whether the decision in *Rogers v Whitaker* was as progressive as it seemed. Justices Dawson and Toohey, referring to the High Court's judgment in *Rogers*, stated that:

> ...the decision affirmed that ... it is a matter of judgment for the doctor to determine what the patient should know in his or her best interests. It was pointed out that in making that judgment the doctor is required to exercise reasonable skill and care and that the court would determine for itself whether that standard was observed ... Nevertheless it was held that it is a judgment to be made by the doctor, notwithstanding that in the particular context of the revelation of the risks inherent in proposed treatment all relevant information to enable the patient to make a decision to undergo the treatment would ordinarily be required ... the decision also rejected the notion of "the patient's right of self-determination" as providing any real assistance in the "balancing process that is involved in the determination of whether there has been a breach of the duty of disclosure" ' (at 278,290).

And, again, the seemingly progressive 1998 Australian High Court case *Chappel v Hart* [21] can be interpreted as compounding these doubts. Beryl Hart claimed that she had expressed concern about the risk of damage to her vocal cords associated with recommended surgery, that the surgeon had failed to warn her of this known risk, and that the risk materialised post-operatively. Again, the issue of question-asking was addressed directly by the Court. Justice Kirby drew attention to:

> ...the duty which all health care professionals in the position of Dr Chappel must observe: the duty of informing patients about risks, answering their questions candidly and respecting their rights ... (at para 95).

Kirby also added: 'This was not an ordinary patient. It was an inquisitive, persistent and anxious one who was found to have asked a particular question to which she received no proper answer' (at para 99). Would Beryl Hart have succeeded if she had not expressed concern about a specific risk?

Furthermore, this apparent assumption that the client is responsible for making sure that they receive the information they need in order to make an informed choice is inconsistent with the common claim by medical practitioners that people do not understand even the most basic medical information. This last claim is then frequently presented as justification for withholding that information. But, if clients have so little understanding of what their practitioner tells them, how can they, at the same time, be so well-informed about medical matters that they know exactly what questions to ask? As McLean and McKay (1981, p.101) point out, the medical community cannot simply change their argument to suit their own needs in different situations.

Standards of Disclosure and the United Kingdom

As noted earlier, English courts have consistently relied on the *Bolam* principle, or practitioner-based standard, as the test for medical negligence involving information disclosure. In *Bolam,* Justice McNair made it particularly easy for a defendant medical practitioner to succeed when he allowed that: '...there may be one or more perfectly proper standards; and if a medical man [*sic*] conforms with one of these then he is not negligent' (at 121). Consequently, in *Chatterton v Gerson*, in 1981, where the plaintiff claimed that she had not been warned of the risks involved in surgical intervention for the relief of chronic pain, she: '...did not get over the first obstacle because the judge decided the defendant had acted in accord with a responsible body of medical opinion' (O'Sullivan, p.83).

Lord Denning had also stated adamantly in 1980, in *Whitehouse v Jordan*,[22] that: '...we must say, and say firmly, that, in a professional man, an error of judgment is not negligent' (at 658). Denning was also anxious that the North American legal doctrine of 'informed consent' would lead to large numbers of medical men [*sic*] abandoning the practice of medicine through fear of malpractice litigation (O'Sullivan, p.112).

It is therefore not surprising that, as already noted, the *Bolam* test was followed in the House of Lords in 1985, in *Sidaway v Governors of Bethlem Royal Hospital and Others*. The plaintiff in this case had suffered nerve root and spinal cord damage following spinal surgery, and claimed that these were known risks about which she had not been warned. However, the majority of expert medical evidence supported this non-disclosure as responsible medical practice. Consequently, the plaintiff was unsuccessful. Furthermore, while the appropriateness of the practitioner-based standard to medical malpractice cases involving 'information disclosure' was questioned in *Sidaway*, the issue was ultimately dismissed. While commentators differ as to whether or not this indicates a progressive element in British common law, George Annas (1984) argues that *Sidaway* is clear evidence that British judges are particularly prejudiced against plaintiffs in medical negligence cases. While there have been several challenges to the practitioner-based standard in the lower British courts since *Sidaway*, none have yet been upheld by a majority of judges in the Court of Appeal or the House of Lords (Harpwood, 1996).

Informed Choice: Simply too Complex for the Law?

As noted earlier, a number of bioethicists have been critical of the common law standards of information disclosure, as well as the procedural requirements that confront plaintiffs when attempting to prove causation. These bioethicists argue that the law does not, and cannot, acknowledge the complexity of informed choice as a process of ongoing communication between client and medical practitioner (Beauchamp and Childress, 1994; Beauchamp and McCullough, 1988; Faden and Beauchamp, 1986).

The Practitioner-Based Standard

Bioethicists argue that the practitioner-based standard is ethically unacceptable. If the customs of the medical community are the only test of negligence, then disclosure practices that clients would consider unacceptable will not be legally negligent. The courts presume that the medical community is capable of deciding exactly what course of action, or inaction, will be in the client's best interests. This standard completely denies the client's right to self-determination (Beauchamp and McCullough, 1988, pp.133-134; Beauchamp and Childress, 1994, p.148).

The underlying assumption of the judiciary appears to be that information disclosure involves the same type of judgment as clinical diagnosis and treatment. But, as Beauchamp and Childress point out, a person's decision about whether or not to undergo treatment is a non-medical issue. The weighing of risks is entirely the prerogative of the client, not the medical practitioner (p.148). It is also extremely difficult to see how it could possibly be in the client's best interests to be exposed to potential harm without their knowledge. Justice Robinson, differing from the majority of his colleagues, stated quite clearly in *Canterbury v Spence* that:

> There is … no basis for operation of the special medical standard where the physician's activities does not bring his [*sic*] medical knowledge into play … Experts are unnecessary to a showing of the materiality of risk to a patient's decision on treatment, or to the reasonably, expectable effect of risk disclosure on the decision (at 785,792).

Robert Veatch (1993) also supports the view that concepts of benefit and harm are fundamentally evaluative terms. To claim that a proposed treatment is scientifically indicated simply means that, according to *someone's* beliefs and values, the person who undergoes this treatment will benefit. However, others might very well assess the situation quite differently.

The Therapeutic Privilege

This allows the medical practitioner to withhold information at their discretion if they believe that the client's emotional state indicates that the disclosure of information would be harmful to that person's well-being, *even if they ask specific questions* about a proposed treatment. As already noted, Jay Katz believes that this simply allows the medical practitioner to revert to the practitioner-based standard. Even Justice Robinson, criticised by Katz for perpetuating the *therapeutic privilege* in *Canterbury*, acknowledged that this privilege needed to be carefully defined as it has the potential to '…devour the disclosure rule itself' (at 789). The existence of the *therapeutic privilege* was acknowledged in Australian law by Chief Justice King in *F v R*, where he stated that the medical practitioner's duty to act in their client's best interests '…may justify or even require an evasive or less than fully candid answer even to a direct request'. It was also acknowledged by the majority of the High Court in *Rogers v Whitaker*, although Justice Gaudron stated that she was not convinced that this 'privilege' existed (Skene and Millwood, 1997, p.81).

The 'Reasonable Person' Standard

Bioethicists have also drawn attention to difficulties with the 'reasonable person' standard of disclosure, which requires disclosure of all information relevant to a decision, according to the court's view of what a hypothetical 'reasonable' client would want to know. Therefore, the final decision lies with the court and not the medical community. This means that medical practitioners can be found negligent with regard to the duty to disclose even if their actions conform to accepted medical standards (Beauchamp and McCullough, 1988; Beauchamp and Childress, 1994). While this standard appears progressive, Beauchamp and Childress draw attention to the lack of clarity about exactly what a hypothetical 'reasonable' person would want to know. Given that the concept of the 'reasonable person' has never been clearly defined by the North American courts, how are medical practitioners to make this assessment?

But, is it even possible to define a 'reasonable person' for this purpose? The traditional legal view of the *reasonable man* [*sic*] has attracted a great deal of criticism by progressive jurists. Feminists, critical legal theorists and authors of postmodern approaches to jurisprudence have all argued that this standard inevitably ends up reflecting the values and beliefs of the judiciary (Bender, 1988; MacKinnon, 1991; Douzinous, Warrington and McVeigh, 1991). One example is Patrick Devlin's (1965) claim that the man [*sic*] 'on the bus' represents the reasonable man in society. But, what is it that makes this person the representative 'reasonable' man? Everyone on the bus, while possibly having some values and beliefs in common, will also have other relatively unique views as a result of their specific life experiences. While the court's interpretation is supposed to be what a hypothetical 'reasonable person' would want to know, it is far more likely to simply reflect judicial beliefs and values projected onto the so-called 'reasonable man'.[23] As Sheilah Martin and Kathleen Mahoney (1987) note:

> The existence of non-neutral judicial behaviour conflicts with the common belief that judges are completely objective, disinterested and impartial in all cases. Until recently this exaggerated perception of constant judicial neutrality helped prevent a close examination of some important issues. The fact that judicial attitudes towards equality issues have rarely been scrutinized for discriminatory practices and conduct is evidence of the pervasive hold of this idea ... Most critiques of judicial decisions focus on the logic and sensibility of the legal analysis and its relationship with precedent. Occasionally, the social, economic or policy implications of judgments are discussed and evaluated. Rarely is a judgment or a group of judgments criticized for the conception of society and the stereotypic treatment of individuals they may contain (pp. iv-v).

Proving Causation

As noted earlier, as part of an action in negligence a plaintiff must prove that failure to provide information about the risks of treatment was the cause of the injury. This means that the plaintiff must establish that, if the relevant risks had been disclosed, consent would not have been given, and therefore the injury would not have occurred (Darvall, 1993, p.32). Causation will not be established if the plaintiff's injuries could have been caused by something other than the defendant's alleged breach of duty, or if they would have occurred regardless of the alleged breach of duty (Bennett, 1997, p.51). Unfortunately for plaintiffs, both the medical community and the judiciary appear to discount the plaintiff's credibility when it comes to proving causation. Judgments have frequently gone against a plaintiff even though they have clearly stated that they would not have consented to the proposed treatment if they had been advised of the risks. And yet, once the plaintiff has reached this point in the litigation process it has already been established that they have experienced a negative outcome following medical treatment, the possibility of which was not known to them as a result of the medical practitioner's failure to disclose this possibility.

Given this, the subsequent test for proof of causation used by the courts is an illogical and empty exercise. Pursuing the question of whether the plaintiff would have chosen to proceed with treatment if warned of the risks will not establish that the plaintiff's injuries would, or would not, have occurred regardless of the defendant's breach of duty. Neither the plaintiff nor the court can make this retrospective decision with any certainty, simply because it is not possible to return to that point in time where a choice was yet to be made. A claim as to 'what might have happened if ...' is simply the opinion of either the court or the plaintiff. This does not prove, or disprove, causation according to the requirements of the law of negligence.

The Bioethical Solution: Shared Decision Making and Trust

Ideal client-practitioner relationship models that emphasise the requirement for shared decision making generally represent the practitioner as essentially beneficent. Even Jay Katz (1984), intense critic of the authoritarian medical model, recommends a client-practitioner model based on trust. Katz believes that this is best achieved by encouraging an ongoing conversation between client and practitioner, including an exploration of the reasons for consent to, or refusal of, treatment. Katz goes on to point out that the practitioner should consider very carefully whether it is ethically acceptable to *interfere with* a particular client's choice. But, does this model offer any real solution to the underlying problem? If the medical practitioner still has the legitimate power to *interfere with* client choice then it is difficult to see how the authoritarian practitioner would be restrained from violating the client's right to informed choice. The ultimate decision is still at the medical practitioner's discretion. Therefore, Katz does not manage to overcome the very problem that he is so critical of throughout his writings on medical ethics.

This same difficulty confronts other ideal models of the clinical encounter. For instance, Dan Brock (1991) allocates the role of client advocate to the medical practitioner in situations where the mentally competent, but ill and anxious, person is experiencing difficulty in making an informed decision about their treatment options. But, to claim that the dominant party to a negotiation can act as advocate for the less powerful party is to completely misunderstand the nature of advocacy; the advocate must be completely independent of the negotiating parties.[24] Robert Veatch (1991), who believes that the ideal client-practitioner relationship is a partnership, also focuses on trust and practitioner benevolence; and Edmund Pellegrino and David Thomasma (1998) argue at length for a model based on practitioner beneficence. But, again, these proposals do not provide a solution to a problem generated by essential differences in values, power and privilege between client and practitioner. People seek assistance from the courts precisely because trust has been betrayed and benevolence abandoned. It is this issue that bioethics should be addressing.

Nor are bioethicists necessarily correct in concluding that the law is incapable of dealing with the complexity of ethical issues. The conflict between client choice and practitioner authority *is* resolved by the courts, despite the apparent confusion, but it is resolved in favour of the practitioner rather than the client. These decisions are based on judicial values, and these are, in general, conservative values. It is the value position of the judiciary that is the important issue, not the technicalities of the law. Consider the following comments made by Samuels (1999), President of the [British] Medico-Legal Society: 'It has to be said that the law favours the doctor and the Judge is well disposed towards the doctor' (p.14). Samuels refers to the plaintiff in medical malpractice cases as 'a gold digger' and 'self-abuser', and reluctantly notes that health care clients do have certain rights, 'However unusual, ill advised or foolish or irrational or repugnant the patient may be' (p.17).

Notes

1 I am particularly indebted to the work of John O'Sullivan for essential material concerning the historical development of the North American legal doctrine of 'informed consent'.

2 154 Cal App 2d 560, 317 P 2d 170 (Dist Ct App 1957). Martin Salgo suffered permanent paralysis following translumbar aortography, and sued his medical practitioner for negligent performance of the procedure, as well as failing to warn him of the risk of paralysis.

3 5 Cal 4th 1172, 23 Cal Rptr 2d 131, 858 P 2d 598 (1993).

4 See *Rogers v Whitaker* (1992) 175 CLR 479; 109 ALR 625 (HCA).

5 Trespass to the person can constitute a common law tort (civil wrong), or a criminal offence. The legal reason for a medical practitioner obtaining consent to treatment is to provide a defence against any future criminal charge of assault and battery, as well as a civil claim for damages (Skene, 1998, p.78).

6 105 NE 92 (1914) (NY Ct of Apps).
7 (1967) 61 DLR (2d) 494, (1967) 63 DLR (2d) 82.
8 354 P 2d 670 (1960). In *Natanson,* the plaintiff had suffered burns as a result of radiation therapy following a mastectomy, and sued her medical practitioner for failure to obtain informed consent, claiming that she had not been advised of the risks involved in the procedure. It is also interesting to note that there was a successful battery action in the state of New York in 1973 involving 'failure to warn'. In response, the state legislature, lobbied by the medical community, passed a law mandating use of the tort of negligence and the practitioner-based standard in 'failure to warn' cases (O'Sullivan, p.25).
9 464 F 2d 772 (1972) (US Ct of Apps, DC Cir).
10 Again, in 1980, when the Oklahoma Supreme Court, in *Scott v Bradford* 606 P 2d 554 (Okla 1980), introduced a subjective standard of disclosure, that is, disclosure required by the particular needs of the client as stated by that person, this progressive precedent was not followed by other United States courts (Beauchamp and McCullough, 1988, pp.135-136).
11 (1980) 114 DLR (3d) 1(Can SC), 2 SCR 880.
12 [1957] 2 All ER 118 (QBD); [1957] 1 WLR 582.
13 [1981] 1 QB 432 (QBD).
14 [1985] 1 AC 871; 1 All ER 643 (HL).
15 Unreported, Fisher J, Sup Ct NSW, 11 July 1980; (1984) Aust Torts Reports 80-201.
16 (1981) 93 LSJS 405; 93 LS(SA); JS 405 (SA SC).
17 (1983) 33 SASR 189.
18 (1992) 175 CLR 479; 109 ALR 625 (HCA).
19 *F v R* (1983) 33 SASR 189; *Battersby v Tottman and the State of South Australia* (1985) 37 SASR 524; and *Gover v the State of South Australia and Perriam* (1985) 39 SASR 543.
20 (1996) 138 ALR 259.
21 [1998] HCA 55.
22 [1980] 1 All ER 650 (HL).
23 Bender (1988) discusses the issue of sexism in tort law at length.
24 This misunderstanding of the nature of advocacy is endemic to the bioethics literature.

References

Annas, G. (1984), 'Why the British Courts Rejected the American Doctrine of Informed Consent', *Public Health and the Law*, vol. 74 (11), pp. 1281-1286.

Annas, G. (1998), *Some Choice: Law, Medicine and the Market*, New York: Oxford University Press.

Beauchamp, T. L. and Childress, J. F. (1994), *Principles of Biomedical Ethics*, (4th ed), New York: Oxford University Press.

Beauchamp, T. L. and McCullough, L. B. (1988), 'The Management of Medical Information: Legal and Moral Requirements of Informed Voluntary Consent', in R. Edwards and G. C. Graber, (eds), *Bioethics*, San Diego: Harcourt Brace Jovanovich, pp. 130-141.

Bender, L. (1988), 'A Lawyer's Primer on Feminist Theory and Tort', *Journal of Legal Education*, vol. 38 (1&2), pp. 3-37.

Benidickson, J. (1995), 'Canadian Developments in Health Care Liability and Compensation', in S. A. M. McLean, (ed), *Law Reform and Medical Injury Litigation*, Aldershot: Dartmouth, pp. 5-30.

Bennet, B. (1997), *Law and Medicine*, Sydney: Law Book Company.

Brock, D. W. (1991), 'The Ideal of Shared Decision-Making Between Physicians and Patients', *Kennedy Institute of Ethics Journal*, March, pp. 28-47.

Darvall, L. (1993), *Medicine, Law and Social Change: The Impact of Bioethics, Feminism and Rights Movements on Medical Decision-Making*, Sydney: Dartmouth.

Devlin, P. (1965), *The Enforcement of Morals*, London: Oxford University Press.

Douzinous, C. Warrington, R. and McVeigh, S. (1991), *Postmodern Jurisprudence: The Law of Texts in the Texts of Law*, London: Routledge.

Dunn, I. (1993), 'What should doctor tell you?' *Law Institute Journal*, April, pp. 268-271.

Faden, R. and Beauchamp, T. L. (1986), *A History and Theory of Informed Consent*, New York: Oxford University Press.

Freckelton, I. (1999a), 'Doctors as Witnesses', in I. Freckelton and K. Petersen (eds), *Controversies in Health Law*, Sydney: The Federation Press, pp. 86-106.

Harpwood, V. (1996), 'Medical Negligence: A Chink in the Armour of the Bolam Test?' [British] *Medico-Legal Journal*, vol. 64, Part 4, pp. 179-185.

Katz, J. (1977), 'Informed Consent - A Fairy Tale? Law's Vision', *University of Pittsburgh Law Review*, vol. 39 (2), pp. 137-174.

Katz, J. (1984), *The Silent World of Doctor and Patient*, New York: The Free Press.

MacKinnon, C. (1991), 'Feminism, Marxism and the State', in K. T. Bartlett and R. Kennedy (eds), *Feminist Legal Theory: Readings in Law and Gender*, Boulder, Colorado: Westview Press, pp. 181-200.

McLean, S. A. M. (ed), (1981), *Legal Issues in Medicine*, Aldershot: Gower.

McLean, S. A. M. (ed), (1995), *Law Reform and Medical Litigation*, Aldershot: Dartmouth.

Malcolm, D. (1994), 'The High Court and Informed Consent: The Bolam Principle Abandoned', *Tort Law Review*, July, pp. 81-98.

Martin, S. L. and Mahoney, K. E. (1987), 'Preface', in S. L. Martin and K. E. Mahoney, (eds), *Equality and Judicial Neutrality*, Toronto, Calgary and Vancouver: Carswell, pp. iii-v.

O'Sullivan, J. (unpd), *The Professional Versus the Material Risks Standards of Risk Disclosure: The Appropriate Standard for Australia*, Master of Laws Thesis (1988), Monash University, Melbourne.

Pellegrino, E. D. and Thomasma, D. C. (1988), *For the Patient's Good: The Restoration of Beneficence in Health Care*, New York: Oxford University Press.

Robertson, G. (1991), 'Informed Consent Ten Years Later: The Impact of Reibl v Hughes', *The Canadian Bar Review*, vol. 70 (3), pp. 423-447.

Rozovsky, L. and Rozovsky, F. (1990), *The Canadian Law of Consent to Treatment*, Toronto and Vancouver: Butterworths.

Samuels, A. (1999), 'The Doctor and the Lawyer: Medico-Legal Problems Today', [British] *Medico-Legal Journal*, vol. 67, Part 1, pp. 11-39.

Seabourne, G. (1995), 'The Role of the Tort of Battery in Medical Law', *Anglo-American Law Review*, vol. 24, pp. 265-298.

Simanowitz, A. (1995), 'Law Reform and Medical Negligence Litigation: The UK Position', in S. A. M. McLean, (ed), *Law Reform and Medical Injury Litigation*, Aldershot: Dartmouth, pp. 119-146.

Skene, L. (1993), 'The Standard of Care in Relation to a Medical Practitioner's Duty of Disclosure', *Torts Law Journal*, vol. 1, pp. 103-113.

Skene, L. and Millwood, S. (1997), ' "Informed Consent" to Medical Procedures: The Current Law in Australia, Doctors' Knowledge of the Law and Their Practices in Informing Patients', in Shotton, L. (ed), *Health Care Law and Ethics*, Katoomba, New South Wales: Social Science Press.

Somerville, M. A. (1981), 'Structuring the Issues in Informed Consent', *McGill Law Journal*, vol. 26, pp. 740-808.

Tan, K. F. (1987), 'Failure of Medical Advice: Trespass or Negligence?', *Legal Studies*, vol. 7, pp. 149-168.

Veatch, R. M. (1991), *The Patient-Physician Relation: The Patient as Partner, Part 2*, Bloomington and Indianapolis: Indiana University Press.

Veatch, R. M. (1993), 'Benefit/Risk Assessment: What Patients Can Know that Scientists Cannot', *Drug Information Journal*, vol. 27, pp. 1021-1029.

Wadlington, W. (1995), 'Law Reform and Damages for Medical Injury in the United States', in S. A. M. McLean, (ed), *Law Reform and Medical Injury Litigation*, Aldershot: Dartmouth, pp. 89-118.

Cases

Arato v Avedon 5 Cal 4th 1172, 23 Cal Rptr 2d 131, 858 P 2d 598 (1993).

Battersby v Tottman and the State of South Australia (1985) 37 SASR 524.

Bolam v Friern Hospital Management Committee [1957] 2 All ER 118 (QBD); [1957] 1WLR 582.

Breen v Williams 138 ALR 259.

Canterbury v Spence 464 F 2d 772 (1972) (US Ct of Apps, DC Cir).

Chappel v Hart [1998] HCA 55.

Chatterton v Gerson [1981] 1 QB 432 (QBD).

D v S (1981) 93 LSJS 405; 93 LS(SA); JS 405 (SA SC).

F v R (1983) 33 SASR 189.

Gover v the State of South Australia and Perriam (1985) 39 SASR 543.

Hart v Herron Unreported, Fisher J, Sup Ct NSW, 11 July 1980; (1984) Aust Torts Reports 80-201.

Natanson v Kline 354 P 2d 670 (1960).

Regina v Bolduc and Bird (1967) 61 DLR (2d) 494; (1967) 63 DLR (2d) 82.

Reibl v Hughes (1980) 114 DLR (3d) 1 (Can SC), 2 SCR 880.

Rogers v Whitaker (1992) 175 CLR 479; 109 ALR 625 (HCA).

Salgo v Leland Stanford Jr University Board of Trustees 154 Cal App 2d 560, 317 P 2d 170 (Dist Ct App 1957).

Schloendorff v Society of New York Hospital 105 NE 92 (1914) (NY Ct of Apps).

Scott v Bradford 606 P 2d 554 (Okla 1980).

Sidaway v Governors of Bethlem Royal Hospital and Others [1985] 1 AC 871; 1 All ER 643 (HL).

Whitehouse v Jordan [1980] 1 All ER 650 (HL).

3 Medicine: Beneficence or Enlightened Self-Interest?

Introduction

Medical practitioners have, from the very beginning, claimed that the client-practitioner relationship is one of trust and reciprocal benevolence.[1] Practitioner benevolence, or promotion of the client's best interests, is said to justify practitioner discretion in controlling the disclosure of information in the clinical encounter. The claim that self-regulation by the medical community will ensure protection of the client's best interests is also based on the assumption of practitioner benevolence. Most medical practitioners, although not all,[2] also claim that this dedication to high ethical standards establishes medicine as a profession, and not simply a business venture.

These high ethical standards are embodied in various codes of medical ethics. However, in practice, standards are not stringently enforced and sanctions for breaches, if they exist at all, are generally so minimal as to be ineffective. This suggests that the development of codes of medical ethics is motivated primarily by 'enlightened self-interest': their primary function is to protect the medical community from external regulation of its activities (Siggins, 1996). There is considerable evidence to support this view, as well as the claim that the medical community has not kept their part of the trust-beneficence bargain with society. There is also evidence to suggest that many medical practitioners seem unable to recognise that they are fallible human beings, just like everyone else.

'Beneficent' Authoritarianism: The Core of Medical Culture

W. D. Ross (1930) makes the distinction between non-maleficence, or the duty not to harm other people, and beneficence, or the duty to provide a benefit. Ross claims that the duty 'to do no harm' is distinct from that of beneficence, and is the more compelling of the two obligations (pp.21-22). However, Faden and Beauchamp (1986) believe that the moral duties associated with these two principles should be unified under a single principle of beneficence. They argue that a specific duty of non-maleficence may not always outweigh a specific duty of beneficence. For example, it might be necessary to inflict a trivial harm in order to provide a substantial benefit. To insist that the 'duty to do no harm' must always take precedence cannot allow for this situation (p.10).

For Edmund Pellegrino and David Thomasma (1988) the duty not to harm clients is the minimal level of the duty of beneficence (p.26). The beneficent medical practitioner acknowledges the client's wishes as a means of protecting their best interests, but also goes beyond 'simply respecting the patient's rights',[3] taking this obligation into account without 'capitulating to it' (p.35).

And yet, Pellegrino and Thomasma are ambivalent about their claim for the priority of practitioner beneficence over client rights. At one point they argue that the primary aim of healing is to restore client self-determination. Therefore, to violate client choice is to wound rather than heal. There is also an acknowledgment that the greatest failure of medical beneficence in the clinical encounter is the common assumption by practitioners that the 'medical good' is the highest possible 'good', when clients might assess the situation quite differently (pp.23-25). Pellegrino and Thomasma conclude that, if a conflict of values between client and practitioner cannot be resolved, then the practitioner should withdraw (p.160). And yet, this directly contradicts the authors' earlier claim that the medical practitioner's decision, as beneficence, should prevail *if there is a difference in values* (p.162).

This ambivalence is particularly evident in the authors' interpretation of the 1986 decision of the Supreme Court of California in *Bouvia v Superior Court* (*Glenchur*).[4] In 1983 Elizabeth Bouvia was 26 years old, quadriplegic, and suffering from intense arthritic pain. While she felt that life was no longer worth living, she was not able to end her life without assistance. Bouvia chose to enter a California hospital, asking the staff to provide her with basic personal care, as well as pain relief, while she ended her life by not eating.

However, the medical staff refused to comply. They believed that to do so would violate their duty to preserve life, and involve them in a suicide attempt, which would be both illegal and immoral. At this point, a lower court rejected Bouvia's petition to prevent the hospital staff from feeding her against her will. The court authorised forced nasogastric tube feedings.

Bouvia then requested the superior court to *enforce removal* of the nasogastric tube, promising to take food normally once the tube was removed. But the judge did not trust her to keep her word, and ordered that the tube remain in place. Pellegrino and Thomasma refer to 'an escalating cycle of confrontation, bitterness, and hostility' between client and hospital staff (pp.198-199).

The issue was finally resolved in April 1986 when Elizabeth Bouvia appealed to the Supreme Court of California. The Court held that the nasogastric tube should be removed on the grounds that this young woman was fully competent and that she had a right to refuse treatment. The court emphasised the legal doctrine of the right of privacy, held that the right to refuse treatment is not limited to comatose or terminally ill people, and that whether or not such refusal hastens death is immaterial. After a three year battle with the courts and her medical practitioners, Elizabeth Bouvia's simple request that she be allowed to die in order to end her suffering was finally granted.[5]

But, according to Pellegrino and Thomasma, the Supreme Court's decision was morally offensive in that it 'reduced' the medical practitioners involved 'to mere instruments of the patient's wishes' (p.199). These authors justify their position by distinguishing between people suffering from a terminal illness and those burdened by a chronic disability. If Elizabeth Bouvia had been terminally ill her medical practitioners would have been morally justified in complying with her request on 'quality of life' grounds. And yet, again, this is inconsistent with earlier statements about client self-determination being the primary factor in healing. According to these statements, Bouvia's medical practitioners should have simply withdrawn from their involvement in her care on the grounds of conscientious objection.[6]

Medical Authoritarianism and the Hippocratic Tradition

The underlying authoritarianism of Pellegrino and Thomasma's view reflects the influence of the Hippocratic medical tradition[7] of classical Greece, which remains extremely influential to this day. According to this tradition, the 'beneficent' practitioner is in command and makes the decisions, while clients are expected to simply obey orders (Faden and Beauchamp, pp.60-61). This belief still lies at the core of western medical culture. Obviously, such an approach rules out the possibility of accepting a client's decision about their health care when this *differs from that of the medical practitioner*.

However, the public of the ancient world did not necessarily consider this authoritarianism 'beneficent' (Temkin, 1995). A Roman citizen of the time remarked:

> On my travels it frequently was my lot to experience various fraudulent acts of physicians ... Some sold quite worthless remedies at horrendous prices; others because of greed, undertook to heal what they did not know how to cure. Indeed, I have certain knowledge of some physicians who act so as to prolong diseases which might be driven out in a very few days or even hours, in order to derive an income from their patients for a long time, and they [thus] show [themselves] more savage than the very diseases (Temkin, p.18).

Owsei Temkin goes on to note that then, as now, the demand for dedication to healing the sick conflicted with the medical practitioner's need to make a living (p.18). While opinions vary, some commentators see very little altruism in Hippocratic medicine. What appear to be ethical directives can also be seen as nothing more than self-interest, calculated to create 'a good reputation' and, consequently, a satisfactory income (Siggins, 1996; Faden and Beauchamp, 1988, p.62; McLean, 1999, p.72).

During the Middle Ages the Christian monastic[8] physicians continued to follow the Hippocratic traditions of clinician authority and client obedience. Many were also pragmatic about medicine as a source of income. Henri de Mondeville, surgeon to the French Royal Court in the Thirteenth Century, advised colleagues not to treat those who were 'unwilling' because a 'screaming or fighting' client would be likely to damage their reputation and, consequently, their income. Mondeville's work focused directly on the profit to be made from astute image-management, advising practitioners that:

> Surgery is superior to medicine, because above other things it is more lucrative. To receive gifts or money, a surgeon dare not fear stench, must be able to cut like an executioner, politely lie, and be clever. Preventive measures should be applied only for counselors, lawyers or advocates, and prepaid patients. The sick above all want to be cured; the surgeon to be paid (cited in Berlant, 1975, p.86).

Self-Interest and the Development of Ethical Codes of Conduct

Ian Siggins argues that Thomas Percival's widely influential *Medical Ethics* of 1803 was the first of a series of Nineteenth Century medical codes aimed at protecting the medical community from internal conflict and external threat. Percival discussed issues such as the setting of fees and the need to establish formal levels of seniority within the medical fraternity. He also emphasised the 'benevolent' authoritarianism of the Hippocratic tradition, and saw no difficulty in claiming that a practitioner is not actually lying when deceiving a client, if this is in that client's 'best interests' (Faden and Beauchamp, pp.67-69). Jeffrey Berlant (1975) claims that Percival's trust-building advice was primarily aimed at preventing clients from forming cohesive groups and lobbying for consumer protection. Percival also advised medical practitioners to refrain from public criticism of each other, to actively protect each other, and to restrict accountability for clinical errors to individual conscience, effectively suppressing both internal and external criticism of medical malpractice (pp.70-78).

By the middle of the Nineteenth Century, newly established medical associations in both the United States and England had developed ethical codes that were presented to the public as an assurance of client safety. The American Medical Association, established in 1847, adopted a code of ethics based on Percival's emphasis on the power and authority of medicine. In England, the General Council for Medical Education was established by law in 1858, in order to deal with the problem of 'unqualified' practitioners. However, again, Siggins argues that the real purpose of these codes was to promote a positive public image of the medical community, and, at the same time, protect it from demands for external accountability. The reputation of medical practitioners was particularly precarious at this time.

In the Twentieth Century, medicine continued to claim the 'right' to self-regulation. Codes of medical ethics also continued to assist organised medicine in maintaining its controlling influence over public policy and its monopoly of health care service provision (Siggins). There is also considerable evidence that these codes have not been effective in protecting the public from harm. Ian Freckelton (1996) points out that without sanctions, and strict enforcement, codes of ethics will not prevent members of powerful and prestigious groups from giving in to the temptations associated with their role.

Consider the following situation in terms of practitioner beneficence versus self-interest. In Australia, in February 1998, *The Age* newspaper reported that a 25 year old woman remained brain dead following anaesthesia for an abortion performed in 1994. This young woman was left completely unattended while recovering from the anaesthetic, and was later found to have stopped breathing. The medical practitioner, Peter Bayliss, was found guilty of gross negligence by a medical review tribunal. At the time of the newspaper report it was not clear whether he would be deregistered. Bayliss, through his barrister, complained of the court costs he had already incurred and 'a down-turn in business' due to the adverse publicity. Then he said: '...if I lose, the money is well spent anyway because it is taken into account in the question of sanction.'[9]

Dangerous Illusions: Infallibility and the High Moral Ground

The phenomenon and risks of 'groupthink' have been widely researched in organisational literature. New members of an established group or organisation are drawn into abandoning any reservations they might have about the ethical acceptability of certain practices in favour of group unity.[10] Groups locked into this pattern often consider themselves above 'ordinary' ethics and assume that they are entitled to act according to their own 'special' moral standards. In these situations, codes of ethics become simply one more strategy by which power is centralised. The dominant views within the group are considered beyond reproach and, therefore, above debate (Sinclair, 1996). The 'groupthink' phenomenon is particularly dangerous when it legitimates already existing prejudices.

Western Medicine and Patriarchal Prejudice

Hippocrates' medical school was closed to women. The few women who did manage to practice medicine were confined to obstetrics and gynaecology, although the male medical establishment increasingly restricted this activity until, finally, by the Nineteenth Century, even this was lost (Alic, 1986, p.28). It was not until the early Twentieth Century that women won a hard fought battle to be admitted to western medical schools. But, even so, despite increasing numbers of women practitioners, medical men continue to exclude them from the more prestigious areas of medical practice.[11]

In 1564 the Italian anatomist Borgarucci claimed that: 'Woman is a most arrogant and extremely intractable animal; and she would be worse if she came to realise that she is no less perfect and no less fit to wear breeches than man' (O'Faolain and Martines, 1979, p.134). In Fifteenth and Sixteenth Century Europe the determination of medical men to eliminate competitors led to an alignment with the church in organising the mass murder of alternative healers, accusing them of 'witchcraft'. These 'witches' were mainly women (Sherwin, 1992, p.150).

In the Nineteenth Century male practitioners considered female reproductive functions pathological. Menstruation, or the lack of it, was believed to be life threatening. Menopause was equally as dangerous. Some medical men also claimed that any involvement in public or intellectual activities would expose women to the risk of nervous collapse (French, 1985). And, in addition to the discriminatory surgery of the Twentieth Century discussed earlier, Kay Weiss notes that a leading 1971 medical textbook stated that women *need* pain, and that if they happen to find pain distressing this means that they are not 'resigned' to their femininity (1977, p.213, 220).

Sexual Abuse of Women Clients

At the turn of the century, sexual abuse of women clients by male medical practitioners is a significant problem in the United Kingdom, Canada, Australia and the United States. In the early 1990s public concern led to Canadian medical boards in British Columbia and Ontario conducting public inquiries into practitioner sexual misconduct. In Australia, persistent publicity about sexual exploitation by medical practitioners has prompted clear statements from medical boards about the prohibition of sexual contact between clients and practitioners. In 1993 Barbara Schneidman, then President of the Federation of Medical Boards in the United States, drew attention to the seriousness of this problem in an editorial in the *Journal of Medical Licensure and Discipline* (Walton, 1998, pp.57-60).

Merrilyn Walton notes that it is mainly general practitioners and psychiatrists who develop sexual relationships with their clients, often claiming that they are 'in love', demonstrating a total lack of insight into the exploitative nature of their behaviour. Medical practitioners have also exploited women clients by representing sexual contact within the clinical encounter as 'therapy'. Again, lack of insight into the harm done is not unusual. In Australia, women have been sexually assaulted while undergoing gynaecological and rectal examinations, and some practitioners have given women clients sedatives, sexually assaulting them while they were unable to resist. Women have also complained about inappropriate medical examinations and offensive language during consultations (pp.61-68).

In March 1999 an Australian newspaper published an article about a psychiatrist who had treated 250 women for sexual problems by injecting them with a potentially life threatening relaxant and then sexually stimulating them. In 1993 the state medical board suspended his licence to practice for six months. In 1996 he appeared in a lower court on 16 counts of indecent assault relating to 11 clients between 1982 and 1991, but was acquitted by a judge who held that he had genuinely believed that his clients had consented to his 'treatment'. And yet, in 1993 this psychiatrist had told the medical board that he did not explain to clients that he was going to touch their breasts and genitals after they were drugged, and, consequently, the board found that his clients had not given informed consent. Nevertheless, this psychiatrist is still practising medicine.[12]

In September 1999 an Australian newspaper published an account of a medical board hearing involving a general practitioner who had allegedly sexually abused two women clients who had also been victims of sexual abuse as children. The medical practitioner concerned had been counselling one of these women, aged 18, for stress related to sexual abuse by her father. The practitioner eventually admitted to sexual misconduct with approximately 60 women clients over a 10 year period.

However, this was not the first complaint of this kind involving this particular medical practitioner. In 1996 the same medical board had suspended his right to practice medicine for two years on five counts of sexual misconduct. In April 1999 he was convicted on charges of indecent assault against eight women clients. He spent three months in jail. At the time of the newspaper report no decision had yet been taken by the medical board as to whether or not he should be deregistered.[13]

As several commentators have made clear, the power imbalance between clients and practitioners means that whether the sexual misconduct involves assault, or a claimed 'loving relationship', or 'therapy', the moral offence is the same. Practitioners are abusing their client's trust and vulnerability by putting their own interests first. Any apparent consent to sexual contact by clients is completely meaningless given the undue influence that a medical practitioner enjoys within this relationship (Walton, pp.56-60; Sherwin, 1992; Wolf, 1996; Brody, 1992, pp.26-27).

Illusory Claims: Certainty and Objectivity

Medicine's claim to the certainty of specialist knowledge is also unjustifiable. Ray Moynihan (1998) points out that one of the most widespread misunderstandings in the general community is that medical interventions have all been proven effective before they are applied in clinical practice.[14] In fact, the majority of medical treatments have not been rigorously scientifically tested (p.5). As far back as 1979, Richard Taylor published a work entitled *Medicine Out of Control,* in which he strongly criticised the use of unproven tests, treatments and technologies by a group that he saw as pre-occupied with its own status, wealth and prestige (cited in Moynihan, p.12).

Nevertheless, as Moynihan goes on to point out, a small group of practitioners are attempting to solve this problem by developing an evidence-based approach to medicine (p.213). This requires clinicians to make treatment decisions based on rigorous scientific evidence, rather than unsubstantiated opinions or information provided by drug company representatives. This progressive movement also takes the unprecedented step of working directly with client representatives (pp.13-15). Obviously, this means that people will be better informed about proposed treatment options.

But what *is* rigorous scientific evidence? As Moynihan notes, research results published in scientific journals vary considerably in quality (p.222). Nor are the results of a single research study a sufficient guide to the safety and effectiveness of a particular treatment strategy, even if the research has been carried out in strict compliance with the scientific method. Research results must be reproduced a number of times before any generalisations can be made. As Derek Gjertsen (1989) explains, a single experiment, or clinical trial, is only the beginning of the process of empirical demonstration, not the end (pp.190ff).

Supporters of evidence-based medicine therefore claim that systematic reviews of a number of studies related to a particular treatment strategy provide the most reliable evidence of efficacy and safety. The small number of reviews that have already been carried out support this claim. These reveal that some commonly used treatments are not as effective as they were thought to be, some are completely ineffective, and others are actually harmful (Moynihan, pp.216-217).

However, despite the progressive nature of the evidence-based approach, a 1998 Australian study revealed that many practitioners were not utilising the evidence provided by systematic reviews, considering this an attack on their 'clinical freedom' (p.220). But how can medical practitioners justify giving their 'clinical freedom' priority over client safety? Roy Harvey believes that this claim is often used to mask a lack of knowledge, as well as to avoid accountability (cited in Moynihan, p.233).

But, even if the entire medical community accepted the evidence-based approach,[15] medicine as a discipline would still have to deal with some strong challenges to its claim that medical science is rational and objective. Gjertsen points out that the rise of empirical science in the Seventeenth Century was not based on proof of efficacy, but on the influence of socially powerful men in socially powerful institutions. The founders of the English Royal Society and the French *Academie des Sciences* defined what was to count as rational thought, refusing to acknowledge dissenting views. Institutionalised science has preserved this authority, and monopoly, by continuing to deny competitors a fair hearing (pp.159-160).

Major critics of the claim that empirical science is objective include Twentieth Century philosophers Paul Feyerabend and Thomas Kuhn, and the mathematician Henri Poincare. Kuhn points out that numerous scientific theories of the past have been accepted as coherent and 'true', only to be falsified at a later date; and that scientists generally interpret, and often consciously adjust, their results to fit their theories (cited inGjertsen). Recent reviews of Newtonian physics, Ptolemaic astronomy and nuclear physics have also shown that even the most 'eminent' scientists have altered observational and experimental data to meet the requirements of their theory.[16] Gjertsen concludes that cultural and intellectual values, as well as personal ambition, significantly influence scientific practice (pp.245-257).

Scientific Fraud

Stephen Lock and Frank Wells (1993) identified 46 major instances of scientific fraud between 1975 and 1993 in the United States, the United Kingdom, Australia and Switzerland. These cases all involved previously reputable researchers from highly reputable universities (cited in Walton, pp.91-92). In 1997 a leading British obstetrician was deregistered after publishing two papers describing work that did not take place, a Scottish authority on chronic fatigue syndrome was accused of fabricating research results, and several AIDS studies in the United States were withdrawn after allegations of fraud. Richard Smith, writing in 1977 as Editor of the *British Medical Journal*, believes that the customary review of a researcher's work by medical colleagues cannot guarantee that fraudulent work will be detected.[17]

Practitioner Competence

Practitioner competence is also a significant concern (Walton, pp.137-138). *The Australian* newspaper of 2 December 1999 reported that 'Basic medical errors, such as indecipherable prescriptions, have been blamed for killing more people in the US than road accidents or AIDS, in a report by the National Academy of Sciences.' This report claims that the death rate from medical errors in hospitals in the United States is between 44,000 and 98,000 people each year.[18]

The *Quality in Australian Health Care Study*, published in 1995, indicated that 16.6 per cent of Australians admitted to hospital in 1992 suffered an adverse event as a result of their health care management. Of these, 13.7 per cent suffered a permanent disability, and 4.9 per cent died. It was estimated that 51 per cent of these adverse events were preventable (Wilson, Runciman, Gibberd, Harrison, Newby and Hamilton, 1995). In 1997, Wilson and Harrison, writing in the *Medical Journal of Australia*, expressed their concern that no action had as yet been taken on the recommendations of the Task Force on Quality in Australian Health Care.

The *Harvard Medical Practice Study*, published in 1991, involved a review of 30,195 hospital records in New York State and revealed a rate of adverse events of 3.7 per cent, significantly less than the Australian figure. And yet, applying these results to the total population of the United States, the authors concluded that medical injury accounts for more deaths than all other types of accidental death combined (cited in Bennett, 1997, pp.69-70). Nor is medically induced illness and death a new problem. This was well documented in the 1970s by Ivan Illich (1976) in his widely read work *Limits to Medicine*.

All this makes the secrecy surrounding Australian health care complaints procedures an issue of public concern. In Canada, complaints are publicly reported, and competency problems dealt with by means of specific programs (Walton, pp.150-151). In the United States legislation passed in 1986 established a national Practitioner Data Bank, accessible to medical boards, in an attempt to contain the costs of medical malpractice litigation (p.153).

While the Australian Competition and Consumer Commission endorsed the introduction of 'performance report cards' for hospitals and medical practitioners in October 1999, an appropriate system has yet to be devised.[19] This may well be opposed by the Australian Medical Association, which has a history of resistance to the introduction of competency programs (Walton, p.161). But, how can this resistance possibly be justified given the high incidence of preventable adverse events?

In June 1999 an Australian newspaper reported that a medical specialist was facing possible criminal charges after injecting 22 clients with a dye containing phenol, a toxic substance used to deaden nerves in instances of chronic pain, while carrying out tests for blocked bile ducts. He had used the wrong dye. And yet, the ampoules containing phenol were clearly labelled. At the time of the report, two people had died, and four were seriously ill in hospital. The medical practitioner had withdrawn from practice at the hospital where the 'medical accident' had occurred, although he was continuing to treat clients at his consulting rooms. The New South Wales Department of Health had referred the matter to the coroner to determine whether or not there was a link between the two deaths and the injection of the wrong dye. One death had been recorded as the result of a brain haemorrhage, the other as the result of a stroke.[20]

On 8 August 2000 an Australian broadsheet newspaper devoted an entire page to an article about the numerous allegations of medical malpractice involving the King Edward Memorial Hospital in Perth. More than 100 couples are currently suing the hospital, alleging that their babies were injured at birth, or died, as a result of medical malpractice. The death of a premature baby in March 2000 has become the subject of a coronial inquest.

A preliminary investigation concluded that 'the incidence of poor obstetric outcomes at King Edward is above the national benchmark'. In 1999 there were 102 stillbirths, three times the national average. Serious questions were raised about the clinical competence of the head of obstetrics, Brian Roberman. The report noted 'with great concern' that Roberman's name was associated with the care of most of the obstetric cases that resulted in adverse events over the past few years. Midwives at the hospital were said to have kept a secret register of babies born dead or injured, given that there was no formal system in place for reporting neonatal deaths and other adverse events.

Maxine Drake, of the Western Australian Health Consumers' Council, believes that: 'There was a culture established for the handling of adverse events, which was to buy out the complaints and bury the complainants; there would be a secrecy clause with every settlement which prevented any public discussion of what was happening.' A hospital board member, speaking anonymously, immediately thought of the parallels with the 'Bristol Case' in the United Kingdom.

Roberman's response to all this was to claim that: 'Our figures are better than theirs [other hospitals]'. And: 'we have women who ... write letters of complaint: "I didn't want an episiotomy (a surgical cut to prevent tearing during childbirth), and I've got a tear and I've got a sore bum," things like that. And this to me is not serious.' The Western Australian government has appointed a second inquiry. This inquiry has the powers of a royal commission.[21]

Illusory Claims to a Monopoly on Healing

Nor can the medical community justify their claim to an overall monopoly on effective healing. The greatest improvements in health during the Twentieth Century were the result of advances in public health measures, which, in turn, resulted in higher standards of hygiene, housing and sanitation (Fisher, 1986, pp.134ff). Ted Marmor (1999) points out that while the Japanese have become the healthiest population in the world at the turn of the century, this has been the result of improvements in the general standard of living following the Second World War, rather than any changes in medical care (pp.262-263).

Even more interesting is the fact that health care spending in Japan in 1991 was the opposite of what might be expected, given the improvements in health standards. In that year Japan spent 6.8 per cent of GDP on health care, Canada spent 10 per cent and the United States 13.2 per cent. And yet, Japan's infant mortality rate was only 4.6 per 1,000 live births, while that of Canada was 6.8, and the United States had the highest at 9.1 (Lavis and Sullivan, 1999, p.315).

This connection between standards of health and standards of living has also been demonstrated in the United Kingdom. The hope that the National Health Service, introduced in 1948, would result in a higher standard of health for the disadvantaged has not been realised. A 1979 Royal Commission found, instead, that it is the upper classes that have benefited. The 1980 *Black Report* attributed the main cause of this health differential between classes to socio-economic factors. The *Canadian Health Reform Report* of 1997 also made the same connection between inequalities in standards of health and socio-economic disadvantage (Mustard, 1999, pp.338-339). It seems then, that despite the major technological changes of the Twentieth Century, overall, medicine cannot claim that it has had a major role in improving standards of health.

Medicine and the Pursuit of Profit: An Inevitable Conflict of Interests

The rapid commercialisation of medicine has been openly debated in the United States since the beginning of the 1980s. However, in Australia, although there were several government inquiries and reports in the mid-1980s, these came to nothing (Walton, 1998, p.37). As Moynihan points out, more and more medicine is business on a corporate scale. Multi-national corporations make vast profits selling testing equipment, pharmaceuticals and other medical technologies. These companies spend enormous amounts of money aggressively promoting their latest products to medical practitioners at all levels (pp.7-8).

Medicine and the Pharmaceutical Industry

The medical community is seriously compromised by the acceptance of extensive sponsorship from multi-national pharmaceutical corporations for ongoing medical education, as well as direct payments for advising these corporations on the promotion of new drugs. Many of Australia's most reputable medical specialists receive regular payments in return for marketing advice, as well as 'free' national and international trips in return for promoting the company's products.

A highly compromising conflict of interests situation exists where medical specialists claim to be offering independent advice to colleagues, clients and the general public about particular drugs, while accepting money directly from the drug companies marketing these same medications. This practice is now so widespread that the Chair of the Australian Drug Evaluation Committee claimed in 1997 that it was becoming increasingly difficult to find truly independent specialists to assist in the evaluation of new drugs (Moynihan, p.8). It would seem that *this* is the real concern with regard to 'clinical freedom'.

Economic Fraud and Greed

In 1993 John Germove referred to a recent Australian Auditor-General's report entitled *Medifraud and Excessive Servicing,* which estimated the extent of medical fraud and overservicing to be more than AU$500 million each year (Germove, 1993, p.6). The United States Government Accounting Office estimated in 1992 that about US$70,000 million, or approximately 10 per cent of the total health care budget, was wasted on medical fraud. British estimates put the cost of medical defrauding of the National Health Service at about AU$400 million a year (Walton, p.40).

In 1985, in Australia, the Commonwealth Joint Committee of Public Accounts, stated that: 'Medical entrepreneurs usually, but not always, appear to work just within the bounds of the law, pay lip service to professional ethics and vigorously scrutinise regulatory measures for loopholes' (Walton, p.40). Moynihan claims that these medical practitioners are becoming millionaires at the expense of the public purse (p.170). While one in two Australian adults live on less than AU$15,000 annually, many medical practitioners earn at least 10 times that amount. The 1994 *Baume Report* revealed that the top 25 per cent of specialist surgeons in Australia were earning more than $500,000 a year, subsidised by public and private medical insurance schemes. The *Report* concluded that this was totally unjustifiable (cited in Moynihan, pp.187-188).

Moynihan also claims that some profit hungry practitioners maximise their income at the risk of their clients' health. People may undergo potentially dangerous investigations or surgery that they do not actually need (pp.10,35-38). In a submission to the Australian Public Accounts Committee, the Hospital Contribution Fund claimed that overservicing has become so widespread that practitioners accept it as 'a style of practice management in Australia rather than as a dimension of anti-social behaviour' (Grabosky and Sutton, 1990, pp.78-79). Economic greed on the part of medical practitioners became so unmanageable in the United States that the government finally took action and introduced 'managed care', which places specific external constraints on the provision of medical services (Moynihan, pp.190-191).

In December 1999 *The Australian* newspaper reported that:

> Up to 250 of Australia's radiologists - a quarter of the lucrative profession - face prosecution in the biggest fraud investigation in the 25-year history of Medicare. The scope of the MRI scans scam, in which radiologists allegedly attempted to defraud the commonwealth, was revealed yesterday in a long-awaited Health Insurance Commission inquiry.

Radiologists ordered new MRI machines, at a cost to the public purse of AU$3 million each, just before the release of a commonwealth budget allowing Medicare rebates for MRI services. Each MRI service meant a fee of AU$475. Allegations of the abuse of 'insider knowledge' were made. At the time of the newspaper reports Australian radiologists already earned between AU$200,000 and $700,000 annually.[22] And yet, after an initial flurry of publicity, little more was heard.

Grabosky and Sutton (1990) claim that where there is no effective regulation, as well as a low likelihood of detection and minimal imposition of sanctions, an increase in corporate crime will follow. They argue that a great deal of medical fraud is the direct result of the structure of organised medicine, the socialisation and training of medical practitioners, and a medical marketplace that creates conditions conducive to fraudulent behaviour (pp.xiv,76). Paul Wilson, Duncan Chappell and Robyn Lincoln (1986) express similar views with regard to medical fraud and overservicing in Canada.

While organised medicine continues to insist that it is ethically superior to a business venture (Buchanan, 1996, p.129), the core question is not whether the practice of medicine is a business or a so-called 'profession',[23] but whether this enterprise is conducted in an ethical manner. Not surprisingly, the literature on business ethics addresses many of the same issues that have been discussed above, including corporate social responsibility, undue consumer risk, disclosure of information in relation to sales, and self-regulation as self-protection (Beauchamp and Bowie, 1997; Coady and Sampford, 1993; Maitland, 1997).

George Bernard Shaw noted in the preface to his 1906 play *The Doctor's Dilemma:*

> That any sane nation, having observed that you could provide for the supply of bread by giving bakers a pecuniary interest in baking for you, should go on to give a surgeon a pecuniary interest in cutting off your leg, is enough to make one despair of political humanity. But that is precisely what we have done. And the more appalling the mutilation, the more the mutilator is paid (Shaw, 1971, p.9).

Notes

1 I am particularly indebted to the work of Ray Moynihan and Merrilyn Walton, which has been an invaluable guide to the writing of this chapter.

2 For example, the Private Doctors Association of Australia openly promotes professional self-interest. Supporters of the marketplace approach to health care do not consider the commercialisation of medicine an ethical problem. Medical knowledge is to be sold in the marketplace on terms set by the owner of that knowledge (Walton, pp.27-28).

3 While these authors acknowledge that the client rights movement in the United States in the 1960s was an understandable reaction to exploitation by medical practitioners of their advantages of class, power and authority, they condemn the adversarial approach of the rights movement as destructive in that it simply 'stimulates scrutiny of abuses of power' without achieving anything positive (pp.14-16,37).

4 225 Cal. Rptr 297 (Cal. App 2 Dist 1986).

5 In the United States in 1994 the State of Oregon passed legislation allowing assisted suicide in certain circumstances. However, in *Lee v State of Oregon* (1995) Civil No 94-6467-Ho D Ore, the judge held that this legislation was unconstitutional. In 1997 in the United States Supreme Court, in *Quill v Vacco: Compassion in Dying* (*Gluckberg v Washington*) 117 S Ct 2293 (1997), the court held that while prohibition of assisted suicide did not violate the Equal Protection Clause of the Fourteenth Amendment to the United States Constitution, assisted suicide was an issue that required further community debate. This meant that individual states were free to make their own decisions on this issue. Later in the same year Oregon re-affirmed its commitment to its 1994 legislation. In the 1993 Canadian case *Rodriguez v British Columbia* (*Attorney General*) (1993) 107 DLR (4th) 342, Sue Rodriguez, a woman in her early 40s,

suffering from a progressive neurological condition, petitioned the Supreme Court to hold that the *Canadian Charter of Rights and Freedoms* allowed her the right to medical assistance in dying when she reached the point of intolerable indignity but was physically unable to end her life. Her appeal was unsuccessful (McLean, 1999, pp.156-157).

6 The issue of the practitioner's right to self-determination in the clinical encounter has been discussed at length in the relevant literature. Clearly, it would be wrong to expect a practitioner to comply with a client's request if this required the practitioner to act contrary to the dictates of their own conscience. Therefore, when a practitioner has a conscientious objection to a client's request they should disengage constructively from the clinical relationship, making sure that the client has access to ongoing medical services if that is their wish. For a clear account of this view see Blustein (1993).

7 This is the Hippocratic model of the clinical encounter, which originated in classical Greece and remains highly influential to this day. By the Fifth Century BC the ancient mixture of magic and religion practised as healing in the Greek temples of Asklepios was already being discarded under the influence of the early Greek philosophers and their search for natural, as opposed to supernatural, causes. Hippocrates taught a medicine based on natural knowledge, observation of the person in their environment, the importance of the skill of the practitioner, and 'beneficent' authoritarianism (Siggins, 1996). The Corpus Hippocraticum, or Hippocratic Collection, consisted of approximately 60 medical works attributed mainly to Hippocrates (Faden and Beauchamp, 1986, pp.53-113)

8 Siggins argues that the most powerful religious code of the Middle Ages, the monastic rule of poverty, chastity and obedience, demonstrated two recurring features of such codes: the significant variation between actual behaviour and the code's prescriptions; and the power of an established code to foster and maintain the preferred social image of the professing group.

9 *The Age*, 18 February 1998.

10 A particularly disturbing example is the continued collusion of medical practitioners in overlooking police torture in developing countries. Practitioners assist police by witnessing the police version of events and issuing false medical reports after examining victims of torture. A survey by the Indian Medical Association showed that 70 per cent of practitioners thought that torture was both required and understandable (Kumar, 1999; British Medical Association, 1992).

11 See for example, Rosemary Pringle (1998). While Pringle provides a searching analysis of the power strategies that patriarchal medicine has employed to keep women practitioners out of the 'men's club', she is also hopeful that women in medicine will manage to bring about significant changes in the next phase of their push for equal opportunity in this field.

12 *The Age*, 27 March 1999.

13 *The Age,* 8 September 1999.

14 A study commissioned by the United States Government in the late 1970s estimated that only a small percentage of medical interventions had been adequately tested. In 1994 the United States Office of Technology Assessment re-affirmed this earlier finding, suggesting that a fair estimate would be around 10 to 20 per cent (cited in Moynihan, 1998, p.5).

15 One of the strongest objections to evidence-based medicine is that it places too great an emphasis on those aspects of medical practice that can be measured, and devalues other

aspects of the clinical encounter. But, as Moynihan (1998) points out, the supporters of evidence-based medicine do not deny that using the best scientific evidence is only one aspect of medical practice. Integrating scientific evidence with both clinical experience and compassion is also central to this approach (p.237).

16 That is, scientists are culture-bound human beings whose choices are influenced by their values, just like everyone else (Wertheim, 1995, pp.9ff).

17 *The Age Weekend Magazine*, 25 October 1997.

18 *The Australian*, 2 December 1999.

19 *The Weekend Australian*, 23-24 October 1999.

20 *The Age*, 17 June 1999.

21 *The Age*, 8 August 2000.

22 *The Australian*, 24 & 25-26 December 1999.

23 According to Buchanan (1996), a profession must demonstrate the following: special knowledge of a practical kind, the application of which is the distinctive activity of that profession; a commitment to preserving and enhancing that special knowledge; a commitment to achieving practice excellence; an intrinsic and dominant commitment to serving others on whose behalf the special knowledge is applied; and effective self-regulation by the professional group (p.107). For further discussion of what constitutes a profession, with specific reference to medicine, see Freidson (1970, pp.71-84).

References

Alic, M. (1986), *Hypatia's Heritage: A History of Women in Science from Antiquity to the Late Nineteenth Century*, London: The Women's Press.

Beauchamp, T. L. and Bowie, N. E. (1997), *Ethical Theory and Business*, (5th ed), New Jersey: Prentice-Hall.

Bennett, B. (1997), *Law and Medicine*, Sydney: Law Book Company.

Berlant, J. (1975), *Profession and Monopoly: A Study of Medicine in the United States and Great Britain*, Berkeley: University of California Press.

Blustein, J. (1993), 'Doing What the Patient Orders: Maintaining Integrity in the Doctor-Patient Relationship', *Bioethics*, vol. 7 (4), pp. 289-314.

British Medical Association, (1992), *Medicine Betrayed: The Participation of Doctors in Human Rights Abuses*, London: Zed Books.

Brody, H. (1992), *The Healer's Power*, New Haven: Yale University Press.

Buchanan, A. E. (1996), 'Is There a Medical Profession in the House?' in R. G. Spece, D. S. Shimm and A. E. Buchanan (eds), *Conflicts of Interest in Clinical Practice and Research*, New York: Oxford University Press, pp. 105-136.

Coady, C. A. J. (1996), 'On Regulating Ethics', in M. Coady and S. Bloch (eds), *Codes of Ethics and the Professions*, Melbourne: Melbourne University Press, pp. 269-287.

Coady, C. A. J. and Sampford, C. J. G. (eds), (1993), *Business, Ethics and the Law*, Sydney: The Federation Press.

Faden, R. and Beauchamp, T. L. (1986), *A History and Theory of Informed Consent*, New York: Oxford University Press.

Fisher, S. (1986), *In the Patient's Best Interest: Women and the Politics of Medical Decisions*, New Brunswick, New Jersey: Rutgers University Press.

Freckelton, I. (1996), 'Enforcement of Ethics', in M. Coady and S. Bloch (eds), *Codes of Ethics and the Professions*, Melbourne: Melbourne University Press, pp. 130-165.

Freidson, E. (1970), *Profession of Medicine: A Study of the Sociology of Applied Knowledge*, New York: Harper & Row.

French, M. (1985), *Beyond Power: On Women, Men & Morals*, Harmondsworth: Penguin Books.

Germove, J. (1993), *Getting Away with Murder: Medical Negligence, Informed Consent and Access to Justice*, Working Paper No. 2, Department of Psychosocial Health Studies, University of Newcastle, New South Wales.

Gjertsen, D. (1989), *Science and Philosophy: Past and Present*, Harmondsworth: Penguin Books.

Grabosky P. and Sutton A. (eds), (1990), *Stains on a White Collar*, Sydney: The Federation Press.

Illich, I. (1976), *Limits to Medicine*, Harmondsworth: Penguin Books.

Katz, J. (1977), 'Informed Consent: A Fairy Tale? Law's Vision', *University of Pittsburgh Law Review*, vol. 39 (2), pp. 137-174.

Kumar, S. (1999), 'Doctors Still Involved in Cases of Torture Around the World', *The Lancet*, vol. 354, p. 1188.

Lavis, J. and Sullivan, T. (1999), 'Governing Health', in D. Drache and T. Sullivan, (eds), *Market Limits in Health Reform: Public Success, Private Failure*, London and New York: Routledge, pp. 312-328.

McLean, S. A. M. (1999), *Old Law, New Medicine: Medical Ethics and Human Rights*, London and New York: Rivers Oram Publishers.

Maitland, I. (1997), 'The Limits of Business Regulation', in T. L. Beauchamp and N E. Bowie, (eds), *Ethical Theory and Business*, (5th ed), New Jersey: Prentice-Hall, pp. 126-135.

Marmor, T. (1999), 'The Rage for Reform: Sense and Nonsense in Health Policy', in D. Drache and T. Sullivan, (eds), *Market Limits in Health Reform: Public Success, Private Failure*, London and New York: Routledge, pp. 260-272.

Moynihan, R. (1998), *Too Much Medicine*, Sydney: ABC Books.

Mustard, F. (1999), 'Health, Health Care and Social Cohesion', in D. Drache and T. Sullivan, (eds), *Market Limits in Health Reform: Public Success, Private Failure*, London and New York: Routledge, pp. 329-350.

O'Faolain, J. and Martines, L. (eds), (1979), *Not in God's Image: Women in History*, London: Virago.

Pellegrino, E. D. and Thomasma, D. C. (1988), *For the Patient's Good: The Restoration of Beneficence in Health Care*, New York: Oxford University Press.

Pringle, R. (1998), *Sex and Medicine: Gender, Power and Authority in the Medical Profession*, Cambridge: Cambridge University Press.

Ross, W. D. (1930), *The Right and the Good*, London: Oxford University Press.

Shaw, G. B. (1971), *The Doctor's Dilemma*, Harmondsworth: Penguin Books. First published 1906.

Sherwin, S. (1992), *No Longer Patient: Feminist Ethics and Health Care*, Philadelphia: Temple University Press.

Siggins, I. (1996), 'Professional Codes: Some Historical Antecedents', in M. Coady and S. Bloch (eds), *Codes of Ethics and the Professions*, Melbourne: Melbourne University Press, pp. 55-71.

Sinclair, A. (1996), 'Codes in the Workplace: Organisational versus Professional Codes', in M. Coady and S. Bloch (eds), *Codes of Ethics and the Professions*, Melbourne: Melbourne University Press, pp. 88-108.

Temkin, O. (1995), *Hippocrates in a World of Pagans and Christians*, Baltimore: Johns Hopkins University Press.

Turner, B. S. with Samson, C. (1995), *Medical Power and Social Knowledge*, (2nd ed), London: Sage Publications.

Walton, M. (1998), *The Trouble with Medicine: Preserving the Trust Between Patients and Doctors*, St Leonards, New South Wales: Allen & Unwin.

Weiss, K. (1977), 'What Medical Students Learn about Women', in C. Dreifus (ed), *Seizing Our Bodies: The Politics of Women's Health*, New York: Vintage Books, pp. 212-222.

Wertheim, M. (1995), *Pythagoras' Trousers: God, Physics and the Gender Wars*, New York: Random House.

Wilson, P. R. Chappell, D. and Lincoln, R. (1986), 'Policing Physician Abuse in British Columbia: An Analysis of Current Policies', *Canadian Public Policy*, vol. 12 (1), pp. 236-244.

Wilson, R. and Harrison, B. (1997), 'Are we Committed to Improving the Safety of Health Care?', *Medical Journal of Australia*, vol. 166, pp. 452-453.

Wilson, R. Runciman, N. Gibberd, R. Harrison, B. Newby, L. and Hamilton, J. (1995), 'The Quality in Australian Health Care Study', *Medical Journal of Australia*, vol. 163, pp. 458-471.

Wolf, S. M. (ed), (1996), *Feminism and Bioethics: Beyond Reproduction*, New York: Oxford University Press.

Cases

Bouvia v Superior Court (*Glenchur*) 225 Cal Rptr 297 (Cal App 2 Dist 1986).

Lee v State of Oregon (1995) Civil No 94-6467-Ho D Ore.

Quill v Vacco: Compassion in Dying (*Gluckberg v Washington*) 117 S Ct 2293 (1997).

Rodriguez v British Columbia (*Attorney General*) (1993) 107 DLR (4th) 342; (1993) 7 WWR 641 (Can SC).

4 The Clinical Encounter: Protecting Power and Privilege?

Introduction

It has been suggested that medicine's monopoly of health care service provision is a conscious strategy to access and maintain the privileges associated with social and cultural power, and that control of the client group is essential to maintaining this power. There is considerable evidence to support this view. In addition, people who believe that they have sustained an injury as a result of medical malpractice generally experience great difficulty in obtaining compensation at law. Nor are medical practitioners held accountable, in terms of meaningful sanctions, when negligence *is* established at law. This scenario is consistent across the common law jurisdictions of Australia, Canada, the United Kingdom and the United States. Client advocacy groups continue to lobby for the recognition and enforcement of client rights, but these efforts are generally resisted by the more powerful medical lobby.

Even so, it seems that persistent lobbying for external regulation of the medical community is the only way to bring about a change in the balance of power. Only then can collaboration and shared decision making take place. While both medicine and bioethics appear to share the illusion that medical practitioners are somehow untouched by the flaws inherent in human nature, this is a particularly dangerous illusion.

People Defending Their Right to Choose: Confronting a Powerful Elite

A 1992 Australian study commissioned by the Commonwealth Department of Human Services and Health explored the experiences of 22 people in one Australian state who had suffered an injury, allegedly resulting from medical treatment, and who had attempted to take legal action.[1] One study participant had undergone gynaecological surgery to repair existing scar tissue, but was informed by her surgeon, *after* the surgery, that he had actually carried out a different procedure from that to which she had consented. This left the participant sexually disabled and severely distressed. The surgeon then advised that further surgery was needed to correct the extreme scarring and disfigurement. This woman sought legal advice, but found it unhelpful. There were also major difficulties in accessing her medical record. An approach to the relevant health care complaints service was also unhelpful (*The Health/Medical Care Injury Case Study Project: A Research Paper*, 1993, p.89).

Another participant in the study had to have silicone breast implants removed after a decade of continuing problems. When the implants were finally removed one was ruptured and several fibrous lumps had to be dissected from the breast tissue. The study participant reported that the surgeon who had inserted the implants had performed a 'barbaric and distressing' closed capsulotomy several years before in order to 'break the scar tissue', after which the breast became infected. When this woman requested removal of the implants, the surgeon had replied: 'What in the hell would you want to do that for?' (p.115).

Another woman commented that:

> There seems to be some collusion involved between the doctors and the solicitors. We don't know what is going on behind the scenes. They invited us to come for an out of court settlement, then left us waiting behind the door - he came back at half time and asked us if we would settle for that amount. It is a gambling business ... (p.44).

Overall, study participants expressed dissatisfaction with both the medical and legal systems. They reported difficulty in accessing information that would enable them to establish that a medical injury had occurred, and believed that medical practitioners closed ranks when it came to dealing with complaints. Participants also had to take major financial risks to pay for legal proceedings. People experienced difficulty in finding satisfactory legal representation, felt powerless to influence legal actions taken on their behalf, and were poorly advised about choices regarding the management of compensation sums once they were awarded. Many participants were unable to continue working, or jobs were lost as a result of extensive periods of time away from work.

Others were distressed that the medical practitioner responsible for their injury was not held accountable and was free to continue practising medicine, possibly injuring others.[2] Participants pointed out that the legal process, particularly when it results in an out of court settlement, does not address the issue of practitioner competence, or lack of competence, and whether or not they should continue to practice. People saw this as a matter of justice. They believed that not only should they have been protected from injury but also that the guilty party should not have been permitted to continue practising medicine (p.36).

A key theme of this study was that poor communication on the part of the medical practitioner was often the factor that provoked people into taking legal action. These findings are consistent with those of A. J. Kellett (1987) who argues that legal action is frequently triggered by a practitioner's refusal to discuss a person's injury, attempting to shift the responsibility onto the injured person, and then sending a bill (cited in *The Health/Medical Care Injury Case Study Project: A Research Paper*, 1993, p.79).

Another difficulty that people encountered was that they not only had to negotiate with their own lawyers but were also the target of the defendant's advocates. Phillip and Suzy Gray: 'I understand that they have a job to do but they just looked us up and down with absolute contempt, which was, no doubt, part of the intimidation process.' Many participants also felt powerless to influence the negotiating process, while others felt pressured into accepting out of court settlements that usually involved relatively small amounts of money (pp.43-44). A further source of distress was the uncertainty as to the eventual outcome of claims.[3] All this was endured under conditions of extreme stress, which often exacerbated the person's injury, and sometimes continued for 10 to 15 years.

The authors of the study believe that, given the major obstacles involved in commencing and pursuing legal action, it is highly likely that there are large numbers of people who simply do not have the opportunity or resources to take action following a medical injury.[4] These same difficulties confront victims of 'medical misadventure' in the United Kingdom (Simanowitz, 1995), the United States (McLean, 1995) and Canada (Benidickson, 1995).

Britain's Action for Victims of Medical Accidents

In 1980 the British Broadcasting Commission screened the television 'docudrama' *Minor Complications*, which recounted the experiences of a woman who almost died after undergoing laparoscopic sterilisation, a minor surgical procedure. The gynaecologist did not notice that the woman's bowel had been punctured during surgery. Over the next few days she became more and more ill, complaining of extreme pain. Her complaints were ignored. By the time a surgeon was consulted a large portion of gangrenous bowel had to be removed.

Having survived this ordeal, the woman concerned attempted to find out exactly what had happened in order to pursue a claim for compensation. However, after receiving an 'independent' medical report that did not support the claim of negligence, her solicitors advised that the case would not succeed. Nevertheless, this remarkable woman proceeded to conduct her own investigations, and eventually located a solicitor who was prepared to challenge the existing medical report. Subsequently, the medical practitioner offered to settle out of court.

Arnold Simanowitz (1995) goes on to point out that this was the beginning of a significant growth in the rate of medical negligence claims in England and Wales over the next 10 years, with people now being prepared to reject the authoritarian behaviour of medical practitioners. People realised that they had the right to ask questions, receive answers and be treated as partners in the management of their medical care. They also realised that medical practitioners could be at fault, just like any other service provider, and, if this resulted in damage, then they should be required to pay compensation, just like anyone else.

As a direct result of the overwhelming public response to *Minor Complications*, the author, Peter Ransley, established the organisation Action for Victims of Medical Accidents, hoping to challenge the medical community's complacency about the problem. While it was not the primary aim of this organisation to promote malpractice litigation, it soon became obvious that this was the only way to bring about change. Action for Victims of Medical Accidents gave people a united voice for the first time. Before this, each person had believed, or was led to believe, that their experience was not only an isolated occurrence but that it was somehow their own fault.

Even so, Simanowitz points out that the outcome for victims of 'medical accidents' in the United Kingdom remains highly unsatisfactory. The primary need expressed by the majority of victims is for the guilty party to be held accountable. But, as Simanowitz concludes, the barriers to achieving this remain formidable in view of the resistance of the medical community and the procedural difficulties encountered at common law.

Action for Victims of Medical Accidents Australia

More than 3,000 people contacted this group in 1998. According to the founder, Lorraine Long, people feel that they are 'kept in the dark' about what has gone wrong. Ms Long established the organisation following her own frustrating experiences fighting for a coronial inquest into the death of her mother. Karen Stott, one of the panel of legal practitioners engaged by this organisation, believes that: 'Sometimes it's not so much the mistake but the cover-up that annoys people ... An expression of regret by the doctor involved would not be an admission of negligence ... but would actually stop a lot of litigation.' 5

Statements of Health Care Rights

While the English public came late to voicing their dissatisfaction with conventional medicine, the North American National Welfare Rights Organisation had already drafted a *Statement of Patients' Rights* in 1970. And in 1973 the American Hospitals Association published a *Patients' Bill of Rights,* which included the right to information about diagnoses and proposed treatments. Other statements of health care clients' rights followed.

Health care consumerism was part of the general growth of public agitation for greater regulation of the marketplace in the United States in the 1960s. The American public wanted assurance of 'fair play'. Health care consumer advocacy movements challenged the traditional power and authority of the medical community, particularly given the increasing evidence of problems associated with many medical interventions. Women demanded more considerate and respectful attention from medical practitioners. Many people wanted the opportunity to choose the health care that best suited their needs (Feldberg and Vipod, 1999, pp.53-56).

A similar pattern emerged in Australia, where a number of health care consumer associations were established during the 1970s (Darvall, 1993, pp.7-9). In 1990 the Consumers' Health Forum of Australia drafted a comprehensive statement of ethical principles and legal rights with a view to national implementation. The Health Issues Centre and the Australian Consumers' Association also produced documents addressing the rights of health care consumers in the early 1990s.

The Consumers' Health Forum of Australia included a description of the right to informed choice in their 1990 declaration of consumers' rights:

> I have the right to an adequate explanation, in terms and language I can understand, of:
> * the nature of my ill health and likelihood of my return to good health;
> * the details of any proposed procedures and therapies (eg consultations, tests, examinations, treatment) as well as possible alternatives including
>   - expected outcome,
>   - adverse and after effects,
>   - chances of success,
>   - risks,
>   - costs and availability,
>   - whether the procedure is experimental or to be used in research,

* the results of any procedures which have been carried out and the implication of these results;
* the possible consequences of not taking the advice of the health worker;
* the name, position, qualifications and experience of health workers who are carrying out the procedures (*Legal Recognition and Protection of the Rights of Health Consumers*, 1990; *Consumer Health Rights: A Summary of your Health Rights and Responsibilities*, undated, pamphlet).

In 1994 the Australian Consumers' Council developed a draft *Health Consumers' Charter* for the Public Advocacy Interest Centre. The mid-1990s also saw the Commonwealth Government, and a number of States, publishing charters of client rights that applied to public hospital services and, in some instances, public health services in general (*Review of Professional Indemnity Arrangements for Health Care Professionals*, 1995, paras 8.10-9.5). However, while client advocacy groups remain active, the far more powerful medical lobby generally acts to frustrate easier access to rights enforcement for health care clients.

Consequently, many people are expressing their opinion of conventional medicine and 'the six minute consultation' by taking a significant proportion of their health care business elsewhere. In 1993, in the United States, the number of visits to practitioners of complimentary medicine totalled 425 million compared to 388 million for primary care physicians. Eighty-nine per cent of people consulting alternative therapists were doing so completely on their own initiative. In Australia, 50 per cent of the population use some form of complimentary medicine as a direct result of their dissatisfaction with conventional treatments.[6]

In 1996, Roy Porter, medical historian, commented:

> ...scientific medicine at the cutting edge - medicine led by an elite that sometimes seems primarily interested in extending its technical prowess, with scant regard for ends and values, or even the individual sufferer, where patients are seen as problems and reduced to biopsies and lab tests, no wonder sections of the public vote with their feet, and opt for styles of holistic medicine that present themselves as more humane (cited in Moynihan, 1998, p.13).

People Receiving Medical Care: Consumers, Clients or Citizens?

While Canada's concept of health care consumerism has been heavily influenced by that of the United States, Gina Feldberg and Robert Vipod (pp.55-63) believe that the American concept of the individualistic consumer accustomed to seeking health care in terms of the demands of the marketplace has limited relevance for Canada. According to these authors, Canada's public health care 'safety-net' means that the provision of medical services takes place within the context of reciprocal obligations and benefits between state and citizen. Because of this, Feldberg and Vipod believe that the term 'consumer' is inappropriate in relation to the Canadian health care setting. They prefer the more comprehensive term 'citizen'.

But, even so, surely the essential point is that the terminology used should convey the sense of an independent person with the power to negotiate for what they consider to be in their own best interests. In my view, this does not rule out the use of the terms 'consumer', 'client' and 'citizen' on an interchangeable basis. (However, it does rule out the use of the term 'patient', which both reflects and reinforces the traditionally passive and powerless role of the ill person.)

After all, the common goal is a more equitable distribution of power within the clinical encounter, regardless of the differences in terminology between advocates of clients' rights as consumers and those who consider the provision of medical services to be a state obligation. And, as Marie Haug and Bebe Lavin (1983) make clear, people need the active protection of the state in order to achieve this redistribution of power (pp.10-11). Whether the person in this situation is referred to as a consumer, client or citizen does not alter the core issue, or the overall goal.

The Adversarial Politics of Organised Medicine

Medicine's claim to power is based on the developments in medical science and practice following the Second World War, including the discovery of penicillin, improvements in anaethesiology and advances in biomedical knowledge. These developments were initially welcomed by a public anxious for better health care. However, by the 1960s there was growing evidence of serious problems associated with 'scientific' medicine, resulting in the beginnings of the health care consumer movement in the United States. But, despite the public's desire for significant changes to medical practice, and for participation in the management of their own health care, the medical community continues to claim the high moral ground and the 'right', and capacity, to be the sole judge of its own integrity and value (Siggins, 1996).

Medical Monopoly and the Pursuit of Self-Interest

Bryan Turner (1995) claims that an important function of medical dominance is to preserve and extend access to clients by limiting and subordinating competing occupations (p.152). Jeffrey Berlant (1975) also believes that the medical community deliberately excludes the public from health care policy decision making and, like all monopolies, protects restricted access to valuable knowledge in order to preserve group self-interest (pp.188-202). This means that clients are likely to want more information than practitioners are willing to provide. 'Medical expertise' is also often used as a mask for exercising privilege and power under the guise of advancing the public interest (Freidson, 1970, pp.321-337). Berlant also claims that the medical community encourages trust in practitioners as a way of discouraging clients from forming politically effective consumer protection organisations that might be successful in lobbying governments to regulate medical practice (pp.70-73). Others also support this view of medicine as a self-interested monopoly (Starr, 1982; Daniels, 1984).

According to Stephen Rice (1988): 'The medical profession in Australia wields immense political power. As a lobby group it is unmatched by any other professional group or trade union' (p.100). Lou Opit, Professor of Social and Preventive Medicine at Australia's Monash University from 1976 to 1984, has claimed that the medical lobby in Australia is highly skilled at acting in defence of its own status, prestige and economic power (cited in Rice, p.102).

This powerful group conducted a successful campaign in 1984 against proposed legislation to increase the power of the New South Wales medical board, and when the same state government announced that the Health Department's complaints unit was to be upgraded the Australian Medical Association branded the move 'excessive and provocative'. The medical lobby also objected to a proposal for a client representative scheme in New South Wales. Michael Aroney, then chairperson of the Australian Association of Surgeons, declared: 'We're not going to stand for watchdogs being put in place to deliberately drum up complaints' (cited in Rice, pp.110-112).

Rice also argues that the 1984-1985 Medicare dispute in Australia was about preserving the group's wealth, although the medical community presented it as freedom of client choice. When an acceptable compromise with the Australian Medical Association was eventually reached, a smaller group of specialists held out for even more money, and won (p.100). The Australian Medical Association also opposed the introduction of Medibank in the 1970s. Turner (1995) concludes that these schemes threatened medical dominance, professional independence and fee-for-service arrangements (p.184). Allen Buchanan (1996) argues that organised medicine in the United States also successfully blocked the introduction of national health insurance, seeing this as a threat to its continued wealth, high social status and freedom from external regulation.

The interests of organised medicine have also frequently coincided with those of the private health insurance sector, which also opposed moves to introduce a compulsory national health insurance scheme in Australia (Turner, p.184). In Canada, private medicine and private insurance are currently lobbying for privatisation of Canada's public health care scheme, Medicare (Evans, 1999, p.38). As Norman Daniels (1985) puts it, to claim that the 'ideal' of professionalism is 'neutral' with regard to the socio-economic interests of medical practitioners is to 'put one's head in the sand'.

Daniel Drache and Terry Sullivan (1999) argue that external regulation of the medical community is essential in order to protect collective social objectives, given that private markets appeal to rational self-interest. The assumption that medical practitioners are disinterested, self-regulating groups who can be trusted to protect the public interest is an unjustified one. These authors conclude that nothing could be further from the truth, pointing out that organised medicine in Canada is currently aggressively exploiting 'the pinch of public restraint for private gain' (pp.6-7). As Buchanan (1996) notes, medicine is no different from other skilled occupational groups where clients are at risk of exploitation because of potential conflict of interests situations and these groups are not exempt from external regulation.

Writing in an Australian newspaper in December 1999, Kenneth Davidson, referring to a recently released Productivity Commission report on private hospitals, asks: Why are the vested interests of doctors sacrosanct? The Commission's report argued for deregulation of the private hospital industry in order to encourage greater competition. However, the Commission did not examine available comparisons between public and private hospitals. Davidson believes that this is because most comparisons show that public hospitals compare favourably with private hospitals. Public hospitals take total responsibility for the client so that their care is fully integrated. In private hospitals, responsibility for the client is split between the hospital and the medical provider. Davidson goes on to argue that this last arrangement is highly inefficient, and wonders why the Commission appears to accept this inefficiency without question:

> Is it because the doctors would fight tooth and nail to maintain the separation? Why are the vested interests of doctors sacrosanct and yet, in other recent reports by the commission, the vested interests of taxi drivers in their licences and chemists in owning dispensaries are not? Because doctors are more powerful than taxi drivers and chemists ... The big problem the commission has to get around is the well-documented fact that the supply of medical services determines the demand. The evidence suggests that "over-servicing" is more prevalent in private hospitals compared with under-resourced public hospitals ... But the commission ... infers that it is not supplier-induced

> demand that causes over-servicing, but the lack of up-front fees ... you can see where this argument is going - the discrediting and ultimately the destruction of Medicare. The commission is replaying the same shonky arguments that the Fraser Government used to destroy Medibank in 1976.[7]

The Politics of the Clinical Encounter: Protecting Power and Privilege

While the medical community generally acknowledges client vulnerability, it is assumed that this supports medicine's claim that the practitioner has the authority to decide what is in a client's best interests, including the provision, or non-provision, of information about their medical care. However, this view is unacceptable to those who believe that this simply increases client vulnerability.

Given the multiple conflict of interests situations inherent in the clinical encounter, the medical practitioner is not ethically justified in making decisions on their clients' behalf.[8] While the stresses associated with illness *do* often mean that the client's ability to make a considered and independent decision is temporarily impaired, this supports the view that people in need of assistance in making decisions about their medical care have a liberal democratic right to independent advocacy services.

Rationalising Control of the Clinical Encounter

While medical practitioners generally argue that people do not want, and do not understand, information about their health care, many clients do not share this view. In a 1986-1987 Australian study by the Law Reform Commission of Victoria (1989) only 12 per cent of practitioners surveyed believed that most people understood basic information about their illness or treatment (p.5). However, when clients were surveyed, 86.1 per cent said that they either always, or usually, understood this information. These people were clear about what information they wanted, why they wanted it, and how they wanted it conveyed. Those conducting the survey concluded that: 'Many of the respondents see information as a 'right' with the doctor having a corresponding duty to provide it; they therefore do not believe they should have to ask for information' (pp.32,43,51). These findings are consistent with those from extensive surveys conducted for the United States President's Commission in 1982, along with a number of other inquiries (cited in *Informed Decisions About Medical Procedures,* 1989, p.7).

Brody (1992) also points out that while practitioner's claim that disclosing remote but serious risks will result in refusal of beneficial treatment or investigations, empirical studies do not support this view (p.94). Nevertheless, Brody fails to point out the unwarranted assumption here that practitioners know what is best for the client. Even more surprisingly, Brody goes on to argue that it is ethically acceptable to refer to risks without going into specific details, unless the client makes a specific request (p.96). This displays a complete misunderstanding of the concept of informed choice. In Australia, in 1995, Fiona Tito, Chair of the Health Professional Indemnity Review, remarked in her Final Report:

> Many times throughout the work of the PIR, doctors have said, "but if I give my patients all the information, they make the wrong choices!" ... Such an attitude is an abuse of power and a breach of trust rather than a justifiable use of expertise (*Review of Professional Indemnity Arrangements for Health Care Professionals,* 1995, para 8.5).

Medical practitioners have also claimed that an authoritarian approach is essential in order to promote healing. Clients must have confidence in their practitioner in order to get well. But, confidence is not promoted by keeping people ignorant, dependent and anxious. In fact, there is evidence that people who take an active role in their health care management do better than those who are passive recipients of an authoritarian treatment program (Sherwin, 1992, pp.148-149). It seems, then, that the authoritarian approach to the clinical encounter promotes the interests of the practitioner rather than those of the client.

Susan Wolf (1988) discusses common practitioner strategies for retaining authority in the clinical encounter, beginning with persistent silence. If the practitioner claims that there is only one right course of action, and fails to disclose the range of options available, along with the uncertainties involved in each option, there will be little to discuss. Practitioners also frequently use withdrawal of services, or the threat of withdrawal, as a coercive strategy (pp.197-201). Susan Sherwin (1992) claims that many medical practitioners also encourage anxiety and dependence in clients as a means of controlling the clinical encounter. They then argue that people are dependent on medical authority. Sherwin observes that this is the same strategy and 'justification' that patriarchy employs in promoting the oppression of women (pp.140-143).

The 'Good' Client as Passive and Obedient

A Canadian national survey in 1993 found that most medical practitioners considered clients who asked questions to be 'challenging their authority', 'demanding', 'aggressive' and 'time gobblers' (cited in Feldberg and Vipod, p.58). According to Brody, a comprehensive review of the relevant literature also suggests that practitioners dislike clients who challenge their authority, as well as those who do not openly express gratitude for attention given. Brody believes that practitioners need this display of gratitude to sustain their fantasy self-image of beneficent power (pp.27-30).

Pellegrino and Thomasma (1988) refer to a number of studies that reveal that medical practitioners consider a 'good' client to be one who is willing to suffer, behaves pleasantly, obeys orders and does not complain (pp.99-100). Interestingly, Pellegrino and Thomasma also consider the 'good' client as one who is scrupulously truthful, complies with treatment plans, is non-manipulative, trusting, just, beneficent, servile, courteous, pays their account on time, and demonstrates tolerance of practitioner limitations, as well as the limitations of medical science. These authors consider that failure to exhibit this last virtue 'is often at the basis of capricious and unwarranted malpractice suits' (pp.106-109).

Ironically, these authors clearly expect considerably more virtuous and respectful behaviour from clients than clients have been shown to receive from practitioners. And yet, this 'perfect', totally self-assured, confident client is also the same person that, according to many practitioners, including Pellegrino and Thomasma, is so anxious that they are incapable of making considered decisions about the management of their own health care, justifying practitioner control of the clinical encounter.

Practitioner Authoritarianism as a Cultural Norm

It seems, then, that little has really changed since Eliot Freidson's 1975 study of practitioner attitudes to their work. This study involved clinicians employed in a contractual, innovative service environment aimed at improving the delivery of medical services by eliminating the commercial element (pp.14-17). However, these practitioners deeply resented being seen as providing a service at the client's request. 'It is one of the hardest things for a new man to take - the feeling that the patient can call you and … you are obligated to go and see him [*sic*]…The feeling that the patient has this power under his contract … is a hard thing for some men to swallow' (p.52).

Practitioners also saw 'problem' clients as more difficult to 'brush off' than in private practice, and felt distinctly uncomfortable when expected to deal with conflict within the clinical encounter. People who challenged the practitioner's sense of total control over the client-clinician relationship were considered 'demanding'. One practitioner was 'shocked and outraged' when a client expected them to be on time for a house call. This was a double 'insult' as a 'demand' for a housecall was generally considered demeaning, drawing attention to the clinician's lack of status in the medical hierarchy (pp.44-56).

Practitioners also resisted any request for accountability from the service administrators, insisting that they *must* be trusted as essentially ethical, 'proper middle-class people'. Any suggestion of sanctions was seen as humiliating and quite inappropriate given that practitioners were 'above all that'. These medical practitioners also covered for their colleagues' incompetence, accepting incorrect diagnoses and treatment interventions as 'normal mistakes' (pp.123-128,183,200). Freidson concludes that collegial consensus operated in a way that could be seen as conspiratorial, with the organised group drawing members together defensively in a common front against the outside world (pp.200,241-244).

But, as Emeritus Professor of Surgery, Miles Little (1995), points out, this defensiveness prevents any recognition of complaints as a valuable opportunity to review, and improve, service provision:

> Culturally, doctors are attuned to regard a complaint as a threat. The natural response is to become defensive, to cover tracks and to find reasons to say that the complainant is wrong. Thus doctors lose an opportunity to define the elusive problems that make for dissatisfaction. Until they learn that complaints are an opportunity to examine and evaluate their performance - perhaps the only really worthwhile opportunity - they will go on the way they are, and the gap between the profession and the increasingly informed public will increase (cited in Moynihan, 1998, pp.33-34).

Independent Client Advocacy

Given this profile of the clinical encounter, there is clearly an urgent need for client access to independent advocacy services in the medical setting. It is a commonplace observation that when people are ill they tend to rely on talking issues through with trusted friends or relatives in an attempt to reach a self-determined decision. For example, in Australia in 1997, Ruth McKenzie, a medical practitioner herself, was hospitalised for biopsy of a breast lump, and then bluntly advised by the pathologist, not the surgeon, that she had breast cancer. She was then 'left alone, sobbing, while the surgeon was summoned. After what seemed like a lifetime ... she was stunned when the surgeon arrived ... and proceeded to give her the options as to treatment.' She was in such a state of turmoil that she hardly heard what he said.

Two days later Ruth McKenzie underwent surgery, having decided upon a lumpectomy rather than a radical mastectomy, a much more extensive surgical procedure. This choice was made after turning to a medically trained friend for advice. Ruth McKenzie remembers wondering how anyone who did not have access to such support could possibly have made a considered decision.[9] Given that few people do have access to this type of informed advice, it is the obligation of the liberal democratic state to protect the right to informed choice of medical services by providing independent, third party advocacy services.

Human Aggression: Medicine and Bioethics in Denial

Peter Gay (1994), historian: 'The scars that aggression has left on the face of the past are indelible. Nineteenth Century observers, along with writers from other literate societies, had few doubts that the human is an aggressive animal' (pp.3-5). Gay goes on to argue that every culture, every class and every century develops its own distinctive 'alibis' for aggressive behaviour.

Ambivalence and Projection

The Freudian theory of the construction of the Convenient Other provides for collective identifications, which serve as gestures of both integration and exclusion. By forming communities of insiders it is possible to reveal, or invent, a world of Others, including individuals, classes, races and nations, that it is 'acceptable' to patronise, ridicule, bully, exploit or exterminate (cited in Gay, pp.35-36). This 'projection' of the insider's anger and fears onto the external Other boosts the insider's sense of their own merits and calms their anxieties. The 'discovery' that outsiders possess serious defects gives permission for the insider to think angry thoughts about, and act with hostility towards, the Other. Freud also considered the human mind a battle ground between the forces of love and aggression, seeing love and hate as intrinsically enmeshed,[10] using the term 'ambivalence' to express this tense interplay of opposites (cited in Gay, pp.68-70,531).

Male aggression towards women, noted since the beginning of recorded history, can be seen as both projection and ambivalence. A clear example is the medieval myth of aristocratic male chivalry and courtly love, involving worship of the loved one from afar.[11] While this myth is usually accepted at face value, as presented in the Arthurian legends, the brutal reality is revealed in the work of a contemporary female writer, Marguerite de Navarre. Navarre's *The Heptameron,* first published in 1558, describes numerous encounters between men and women that are saturated with rape and sexual brutality.[12]

Male projection and ambivalence towards women is also evident in the patriarchal institutions of contemporary society, where it is so prevalent as to appear 'normal'. As Susan Sherwin (1992) points out, one of the central insights of feminist analysis is that the danger of oppression is greatest where bias is so pervasive as to be invisible and, therefore, accepted as normal. Sherwin argues that bioethics needs to consider the ethical issues hidden within 'ordinary' assumptions about health care, beginning with the abuse of medical power in the clinical encounter (pp.10,56).

Brody, a bioethicist, acknowledges that, while medical ethics is ultimately about power and its responsible use by the medical community, the word 'power' is virtually absent from the bioethical literature. As Brody points out, to confront the issue of power is to bypass the rationalising and intellectualising defenses of the scholarly approach. Brody then goes on to discuss the human lust for, and abuse of, power, concluding that the emphasis of the medical community on trust and beneficence constitutes a denial of this instinctual human impulse (pp.12,21-22).

Authoritarianism Masquerading as Beneficence

And yet, surprisingly, having acknowledged all this, Brody ends by proposing a client-practitioner relationship model of shared power, focussing on practitioner obligations and beneficence rather than client rights (pp.43-45). Brody also goes on to claim that even though the power differential between client and practitioner is irreducible, the good character of the practitioner will ensure the sharing of power in the clinical encounter. Brody even goes so far as to characterise the rights approach as 'hopelessly adversarial',[13] as do the majority of bioethicists, and abruptly dismisses the suggestion of independent client advocacy as totally impractical (pp.105-109).

This tension in Brody's argument, and the final retreat into what is effectively uncontrolled medical authoritarianism, under the guise of 'beneficence', is the same ambivalence so evident in the work of Pellegrino and Thomasma, discussed earlier. These authors actually admit at one point that: 'Physicians understandably baulk at their reduction to mere functionaries of patient's wishes, just as patients now baulk at their reduction to infantile dependency on physicians' (p.38). While this is a clear admission of the deep, instinctual need of the medical practitioner to retain control of the clinical encounter, Pellegrino and Thomasma do not seem to be aware of this. They go on to make the naïve claim that the 'good' of the client is promoted by means of the integrity and 'good' character of the majority of medical practitioners and that an ethic of rights is both unnecessary and destructive (pp.33-34).

However, it is precisely because the behavioural choices of the medical practitioner are so central to the outcome of the clinical encounter that clients' liberal democratic rights must be given effective legal protection. In general, medical practitioners are still not prepared to share their power with clients. An openly adversarial phase is therefore needed in order to change the balance of power within the clinical encounter. Only then will collaboration be possible. This is a clear example of precisely why liberal democratic societies turn to the rule of law: to restrain the aggressive and oppressive behaviour of flawed human beings.

Notes

1 The authors of this study experienced considerable difficulty in contacting potential participants. There was no official data source on people who had sought compensation involving alleged medical negligence. The Medical Protection Society, which was thought to have the best data, was not prepared to make this available because of the economic implications for their role as insurers. A further complicating factor was that the vast majority of medical negligence claims are resolved by means of out of court settlements. Eventually, the majority of study participants were recruited via newspaper and community organisation advertisements (p.12).

2 The authors cite the work of Marshall (1993) who argues that most victims of medical injuries are primarily concerned about obtaining an explanation as to why their injury occurred, as well as an apology from the medical practitioner involved. They also want to ensure that the practitioner will not make the same mistake in the future (pp.ix, x,36).

3 The authors note that the torts-based system of compensation for personal injury is often referred to as a 'lottery' in the legal literature (p.77). It should also be noted that the most blatant cases involving 'medical accidents' are settled out of court, which means that the details remain completely confidential and cannot be discussed at any level.

4 One participant in this study had not taken legal action because they did not feel comfortable about questioning the medical practitioner concerned, despite the seriousness of their injury. This person, who had not been warned about the known risk of injury prior to giving consent to proposed surgery, was in a particularly vulnerable position as she was dependent on the medical practitioner concerned for her ongoing health care management (pp.27-28).

5 *The Weekend Australian*, 11-12 December 1999.

6 *The Sunday Age*, 27 February 2000.

7 *The Age*, 9 December 1999.

8 Talcott Parsons' influential view of the 'sick role' has been seen by many as an alternative to the constraints of the medical model, an essentially biomechanical view of disease (Turner, pp.9-10,48). According to Parsons' social context approach, society legitimates control of the ill person by the medical practitioner as a means of controlling deviance from social role obligations. The ill person therefore has a social obligation to cooperate fully with their clinician in getting well (pp.38-39). However, this view clearly reinforces medical authoritarianism, although Parsons, along with Emile Durkheim and Max Weber, considered the medical community to be completely above indulgence in self-interest (p.129).

9 *The Age Good Weekend*, 6 December 1997.

10 As Gay points out, psychoanalysts, sociologists and ethologists have been debating the sources of human aggression for decades. Ethologists, beginning with Konrad Lorenz, have argued for an innate aggressive drive that resists modification. However, sociobiologists, along with liberal anthropologists, have rejected this biological determinism, arguing that human nature can be moulded by environmental influences

such as education. And yet, this school of thought has failed to account for those traits that appear to persist, regardless of environmental influences. Others have therefore argued that this is an 'oversocialised' view of human nature (Gay, pp.529-536). This issue is, of course, one of the great unresolved debates of the Nineteenth and Twentieth Centuries.

11 For an example of this traditional literature see Chretien de Troyes (1987).

12 Susan Brownmiller, in her pioneering 1974 work on rape, argues that the act exists at several levels, including emotional settings where hierarchical, authoritarian structures weaken the victim's resistance. Brownmiller also points out that neither Freud nor any of his followers explored or acknowledged the issue of rape, which is remarkable given the importance of the clash between *eros* and aggression in Freudian psychoanalysis (pp.11,256).

13 And yet, elsewhere, Brody acknowledges the need for legal constraints in order to deal with abuses of power by medical practitioners.

References

Australian Department of Human Services and Health, (1993), *The Health/Medical Care Injury Case Study Project: A Research Paper*, Canberra: Australian Government Publishing Service.

Australian Department of Human Services and Health, (1995), *Review of Professional Indemnity Arrangements for Health Care Professionals: Compensation and Professional Indemnity in Health Care, Final Report*, Canberra: Australian Government Publishing Service.

Benidickson, J. (1995), 'Canadian Developments in Health Care Liability and Compensation', in S. A. M. McLean (ed), *Law Reform and Medical Injury Litigation*, Aldershot: Dartmouth, pp. 5-30.

Berlant, J. (1975), *Profession and Monopoly: A Study of Medicine in the United States and Great Britain*, Berkely: University of California Press.

Brody, H. (1992), *The Healer's Power*, New Haven: Yale University Press.

Brownmiller, S. (1974), *Against Our Will: Men, Women and Rape*, Harmondsworth: Penguin Books.

Buchanan, A. E. (1996), 'Is There a Medical Profession in the House?' in R. G. Spece, D. S. Shimm and A. E. Buchanan (eds), *Conflicts of Interest in Clinical Practice and Research*, New York: Oxford University Press, pp. 105-136.

Consumers' Health Forum of Australia, (1990), *Legal Recognition and Protection of the Rights of Health Consumers*, Canberra.

Consumers' Health Forum of Australia, (undated), *Consumer Health Rights: A Summary of your Health Rights and Responsibilities*, pamphlet.

Daniels, N. (1984), 'Understanding Physician Power', *Philosophy and Public Affairs*, vol. 13 (40), pp. 347-357.

Daniels, N. (1985), *Just Health Care*, Cambridge: Cambridge University Press.

Darvall, L. (1993), *Medicine, Law and Social Change: The Impact of Bioethics, Feminism and Rights Movements on Medical Decision-Making*, Sydney: Dartmouth.

de Navarre, M. (1984), *The Heptameron*, P. A. Chilton (trans), London: Penguin Books.

de Troyes, C. (1987), *Arthurian Romances*, D. D. R. Owen (trans), London: D. M. Dent & Sons.

Drache, D. and Sullivan, T. (1999), 'Health Reform and Market Talk: Rhetoric and Reality', in D. Drache and T. Sullivan (eds), *Market Limits in Health Reform: Public Success, Private Failure*, London and New York: Routledge, pp. 1-21.

Evans, R. (1996), 'Health Reform: What 'Business' is it of Business?' in D. Drache and T. Sullivan (eds), *Market Limits in Health Reform: Public Success, Private Failure*, London and New York: Routledge, pp. 25-47.

Feldberg, G. and Vipod, R. (1999), 'The Virus of Consumerism', in D. Drache and T. Sullivan (eds), *Market Limits and Health Reform: Public Success, Private Failure*, London and New York: Routledge, pp. 48-64.

Freidson, E. (1970), *Profession of Medicine: A Study of the Sociology of Applied Knowledge*, New York: Harper & Row.

Freidson, E. (1975), *Doctoring Together: A Study of Professional Social Control*, New York: Elsevier Scientific Publishing.

Gay, P. (1993), *The Cultivation of Hatred: The Bourgeois Experience, Victoria to Freud*, Volume 3, London: Harper Collins.

Haug, M. and Lavin, B. (1983), *Consumerism in Medicine: Challenging Physician Authority*, Beverly Hills: Sage Publications.

Law Reform Commission of Victoria, (1989), *Informed Decisions about Medical Procedures: Doctor and Patient Studies*, Canberra: Australian Government Publishing Service.

Law Reform Commission of Victoria, Australian Law Reform Commission, New South Wales Law Reform Commission, (1989), *Informed Decisions About Medical Procedures*, Canberra: Australian Government Publishing Service.

McLean, S. A. M. (1995), 'Whither Medical Injury Law?' in S. A. M. McLean (ed), *Law Reform and Medical Injury Litigation*, Aldershot: Dartmouth, pp. 1-4.

Pellegrino, E. D. and Thomasma, D. C. (1988), *For the Patient's Good: The Restoration of Beneficence in Health Care*, New York: Oxford University Press.

Rice, S. (1988), *Some Doctors Make You Sick*, North Ryde, New South Wales: Angus & Robertson.

Sherwin, S. (1992), *No Longer Patient: Feminist Ethics and Health Care*, Philadelphia: Temple University Press.

Sherwin, S. (1996), 'Feminism and Bioethics', in S. M. Wolf (ed), *Feminism and Bioethics: Beyond Reproduction*, New York: Oxford University Press, pp. 48-56.

Siggins, I. (1996), 'Professional Codes: Some Historical Antecedents', in M. Coady and S. Bloch (eds), *Codes of Ethics and the Professions*, Melbourne: Melbourne University Press, pp. 55-71.

Simanowitz, A. (1995), 'Law Reform and Medical Negligence Litigation: The UK Position', in S. A. M. McLean (ed), *Law Reform and Medical Injury Litigation*, Aldershot: Dartmouth, pp. 199-146.

Starr, P. (1982), *The Social Transformation of American Medicine*, New York: Basic Books.

Turner, B. S. with Samson, C. (1995), *Medical Power and Social Knowledge*, (2nd ed), London: Sage Publications.

Wolf, S. M. (1988), 'Conflict Between Doctor and Patient', *Law, Medicine and Health Care*, vol. I6 (3-4), pp. 197-203.

Wolf, S. M. (1996), 'Gender and Feminism in Bioethics', in S. M. Wolf (ed), *Feminism and Bioethics: Beyond Reproduction*, New York: Oxford University Press, pp. 3-43.

5 Human Rights: A Problem for Political Rationalism?

Introduction

Classical liberal theorists of the Seventeenth and Eighteenth Centuries argued for the universal right to individual freedom, deeply influenced by the European Enlightenment, which rejected medieval superstition in favour of reason as the ultimate guide to progress.[1] However, the extent to which the liberal democratic state should protect citizens' rights by imposing corresponding duties on others, and so *restricting* freedom to some extent, continues to be debated by contemporary liberal theorists.[2]

Thomas Nagel (1991) supports the view that the state should protect individual freedom, considering this a right in itself. He believes that this is essential in order to protect individuals from the coercive power of the state, as well as from interference by others. However, libertarians, such as Robert Nozick (1974), do not agree, arguing that state intervention should be limited to an absolute minimum.

But, as Isaiah Berlin (1969) points out: '...freedom for the wolves has often meant death to the sheep' (p.165). Berlin also sees a totalitarian threat in the western obsession with rationality.[3] After all, anything can be justified in the name of *the one right view of the good life* (pp.146-152). It is power, and the fact that power corrupts, that places human rights at risk. The illusion that reason dominates human affairs is the source of the failure of both classical and contemporary liberal democratic theories to ensure citizens' protective rights.[4]

Classical Liberalism: Rationalist Illusions and Human Aggression

To the dismay of the majority of classical liberals, the Enlightenment's 'rule of reason' did not survive the violence unleashed by the French Revolution at the end of the Eighteenth Century. Simon Schama (1989) confronts the painful problem of Revolutionary violence, generally avoided by earlier historians. 'I have returned it [violence] to the centre of the stage since it seems to me that it was not merely an unfortunate by-product of politics ... In some depressingly unavoidable sense, violence *was* the Revolution itself' (p.xv). And, while the initial commitment of the Revolution was to *universal* rights,[5] it ended with the exclusion of all women, as well as men without property, from citizenship. This disenfranchised the majority of the population (p.498).

Olympe de Gouges, playwright and political activist, wrote her *Declaration of the Rights of Women and Citizenesses* in 1791. In 1793, at the age of 45, she was beheaded. De Gouge urged women to recognise that: '...in this age of light and wisdom, he seeks to rule like a despot over a sex endowed with the fullest intellectual faculties' (cited in Harth, 1992, p.214). De Gouge argued for equal rights based on natural equality.[6]

According to Article Four of the Revolution's *Declaration of the Rights of Man*:

> Freedom consists in the power of doing anything that does not harm others. Thus the exercise of each man's [*sic*] natural rights has no limits other than those that assure the other members of society the enjoyment of the same rights, limits that may be set only by law (cited in Harth, pp.218-219).

De Gouge responded to this in Article Four of her *Declaration of the Rights of Women and Citizenesses* with:

> Freedom and justice consist in giving back everything that belongs to others; thus the exercise of woman's natural rights finds limits only in the perpetual tyranny imposed on her by man. These limits must be reformed by the laws of nature and reason (cited in Harth, p.219).

And yet, Immanuel Kant, arguably the most revered philosopher of reason of the Eighteenth Century, and generally considered 'the great liberal' within the western legal, political and ethical tradition, could write, 14 years after the Revolution, that: 'It does not matter if the revolution of an intelligent people, such as we have seen in our own time, it does not matter if it succeeds or fails, it does not matter if it piles up miseries and atrocities'. What does matter for Kant is that the Revolution will inspire others to fight for their right to a constitution 'in accordance with law and morality' (cited in Foucault, 1994, pp.142-145).

But, as Peter Gay (1994) points out, the rest of Europe became deeply disillusioned with the Revolution and its horrors. The contradiction between Revolutionary 'bills of rights' and the reality of savage actions was so blatant that all but the most obsessed supporters were shocked and disturbed by these events (p.223).

Nor could Kant's views on the Revolution be more inconsistent with his ethical theory: 'Act only according to that maxim by which you can at the same time will that it should become a universal law.' And: '...every rational being exists as an end in himself [*sic*]' (1990, p.38). People should act so that they always treat everyone, including themselves, as an end and never only as a means to an end (1990, pp.45-46).

Kant and the Limits of Reason

For Kant, the social contract is required by reason. It is not a literal account of the beginnings of political society, nor is citizen consent the grounds for the political obligations of the head of state. These obligations are a dictate of reason. Kant also argued that individual freedom should be constrained only to the extent required to protect the freedom of others (cited in Reiss, 1991, pp.46ff).

And yet, he is extremely doubtful as to the possibility of *actual* freedom. Kant's point is that freedom must be presupposed in order to consider humans as rational. Moral decision making, a rational process, is necessarily informed by the *idea* of freedom. While moral action is largely unachievable in the real world,[7] this is not the important point for Kant. What is important is that 'reason of itself and independently of all appearances commanded what ought to be done' (1990, pp.24,66).

Kant is, in fact, far from optimistic about the human capacity for rational action. And yet, at the same time his idealism takes priority over the reality of the human condition. Consequently, he leaves the way open for the totalitarian state, insisting that citizens are never justified in rebelling against an oppressive regime because heads of state will always make laws that are in harmony with *right* because they have an infallible standard in the idea of the social contract (cited in Reiss, pp.79-83).

Clearly, Kant's argument for *universal* rights is seriously compromised by this view. His insistence on the essential rationality of politics inevitably leaves the citizen vulnerable to rights violations. Kant also compromises his 'categorical imperative' when he claims that although everyone is equal in terms of citizenship, '*the utmost inequality of the masses*' is quite justifiable when it comes to individual possessions, property, the obligation of the poor to obey the rich, and the obligation of women to obey men (cited in Reiss, pp.77-79).

He also believes that all women, and most men, are incapable of acting as rational moral agents because of their essential cowardice. Nor does he have any respect for 'the great unthinking masses' (1990, pp.83-84):

> If he [*sic*] lives among others of his own species man is an animal who needs a master ... For he certainly abuses his freedom in relation to others of his own kind. And even although, as a rational creature, he desires a law to impose limits on the freedom of all, he is still misled by his self-seeking animal inclinations into exempting himself from the law where he can. He thus requires a **master** to ... force him to obey a universally valid will under which everyone can be free (cited in Reiss, p.46).

This clash between Kant's idealism and his observations of the reality of the human condition demonstrates a deep ambivalence about the relationship between reason and the non-rational aspects of human behaviour. He places the fantasy of reason as 'the supreme ruler' at the centre of his work, while he relegates the reality of the human condition to what amounts to a 'footnote'.

Kant also demonstrates a strong identification with the prejudices of an elitist patriarchy. Nor was he alone here. Most other classical liberal theorists displayed a similar prejudice, consistent with the deeply entrenched tradition of Aristotelian patriarchal elitism in western thought.[8] John Locke, Seventeenth Century English philosopher and arguably the first major liberal theorist, claimed, in contrast to Kant, that oppressed citizens *do* have the right to revolt (cited in Hindress, 1996, pp.52-53). However, he did not extend this to the management of the family. While individual rights make absolutist governments illegitimate, the same absolutism is quite justified within the family, where the position of 'ruler' naturally falls to the man as 'the abler and the stronger' (cited in Moller Okin, 1979, p.200).

David Hume and 'Reason as Wisdom'

David Hume, Eighteenth Century philosopher, was one of the few to object to the prevailing obsession with reason.[9] In *A Treatise of Human Nature,* first published in 1790, he argues that emotions are the exclusive motivation for human action, while reason is restricted to abstract thinking. A person might revise their plan of action in response to a reasoned review of a problem, but the initial impulse to act arises from the emotions. Nor can reason distinguish between right and wrong, simply because there are no observable facts involved in a wrongful act. The sense of 'wrongness' associated with a particular action is the result of the feelings of disapproval that it arouses.[10] Hume also saw the necessity of actively restraining the human impulse to abuse power:

> ...according to common notions a man has no power, where very considerable motives lie betwixt him and the satisfaction of his desires, and determine him to forbear what he wishes to perform. I do not think I have fallen into my enemy's power, when I see him pass me in the streets with a sword by his side, while I am unprovided of any weapon. I know that the fear of the civil magistrate is as strong a restraint as any of iron, and that I am in as perfect safety as if he were chain'd or imprison'd. But when a person acquires such an authority over me, that not only there is no external obstacle to his actions; but also that he may punish or reward me as he pleases, without any dread of punishment in his turn, I then attribute a full power to him, and consider myself as his subject or vassal (1971, p.363).

It is also interesting to note that this is highly reminiscent of Kant's observation that 'man' requires a 'master' to force him to obey 'a universally valid will': the essence, in fact, of the liberal rule of law. And yet these two Eighteenth Century thinkers adopted opposing views of the nature of reason and its role in human behaviour, as well as its relationship to ethics. This supports the view that the tension in Kant's work is a result of his insistence in forcing a false dichotomy of reason/non-reason on the 'human animal',[11] whereas Hume presents an integrated view. Ironically, it is 'reason as wisdom' that leads Hume to this integrated view.

Contemporary Liberal Theory: John Rawls' Rationalist Illusions

John Rawls' (1971) Kantian liberal theory of 'justice as fairness' has had a major influence on contemporary moral and political thought. For Rawls, a just society requires a fair system of social cooperation between free and equal individuals, therefore, he begins by setting up a hypothetical device that he believes will guarantee impartiality in choosing the principles of justice. Rawls then assumes that the principles of justice that would be chosen under these conditions are: equality of basic liberties; fair equality of opportunity; and equality of access to resources, although inequalities can be justified if the most disadvantaged citizens receive some degree of benefit. These principles are intended to apply to the basic structures of a liberal democratic society, govern the allocation of rights and duties and regulate distribution of social and economic advantages (Moller Okin, 1989, p.93).

Rawls' Original Position

Rawls' hypothetical device is the *original position*. He proposes that someone in this situation would not be aware of their social position or their natural abilities. They would not be aware of 'their conceptions of the good or their special psychological propensities' (p.17). The principles of justice are chosen behind this *veil of ignorance* in an attempt to promote impartial, rational decision making (pp.136ff). However, this concept has been subjected to a great deal of criticism since its publication in 1971. A major objection is that the description of the person in this situation is a description of someone who barely has any sense of identity, and who would therefore be incapable of functioning at the intellectual and psychological level necessary for choosing the principles of justice. So, even if they *could* imagine themselves in the *original position*, which is psychologically implausible, they would not be capable of carrying out the very task that Rawls has set (Sandel, 1984, pp.163ff).

In reply, Rawls might say that this is too literal an interpretation of the *original position* and that his aim was simply to establish a hypothetical situation that would inhibit the most blatant influences of self-interest:

> The idea here is simply to make vivid to ourselves the restrictions that it seems reasonable to impose on arguments for principles of justice, and therefore on these principles themselves. Thus it seems reasonable and generally acceptable that no one should be advantaged or disadvantaged by natural fortune or social circumstances in the choice of principles. It also seems widely agreed that it should be impossible to tailor principles to the circumstances of one's own case. We should insure further that particular inclinations and aspirations, and persons' conceptions of their good do not affect the principles adopted (p.18).

And yet, Rawls actually goes much further than his initial claim allows when he makes the statement that a participant's conception of 'their good' should not influence their choice of the principles of justice. Again, how can an individual with no conception of 'their good' make a meaningful choice of this kind? Even more confusing is the fact that elsewhere in *A Theory of Justice* Rawls appears to acknowledge the need for an 'integrated identity' if there is to be any meaningful decision making. 'Obviously the purpose of these conditions is to represent equality between human beings as moral persons, as creatures having a conception of their good and capable of a sense of justice' (pp.18-19). This is the same ambivalence so evident in Kant's work, that is, the conflict between the ideal of pure impartiality and rationality and the recognition that this is unattainable.

There is also a problem for Rawls in his prior assumptions about the nature of the task that he has taken on:

> I assume, for one thing, that there is a broad measure of agreement that principles of justice should be chosen under certain conditions. To justify a particular description of the initial situation one shows that it incorporates these commonly shared presumptions ... The ideal outcome would be that these conditions determine a unique set of principles; but I shall be satisfied if they suffice to rank the main traditional conceptions of social justice (p.18).

But just whose 'traditional conceptions of social justice' are these? They are simply Rawls' own views, although he claims that they are universal. He has not been able to set aside his own values and beliefs in his attempt to establish the argument for the conditions of the *original position.* As David Schaeffer puts it, Rawls must violate his own description of the *original position* in order to derive anything meaningful from it (Schaeffer, 1979, pp.30-35).

And yet, despite these difficulties, Susan Moller Okin (1989) defends Rawls' concept, replacing the 'dismembered selves' with participants who will be capable of considering the position of all citizens, in the sense of each in turn, ensuring that the chosen principles of justice will be acceptable to everyone (pp.101-107). It seems, then, that Moller Okin has transformed Rawls' account of the *original position* into one of participatory democratic decision making by real people. However, if this interpretation is accepted, Rawls would not be able to predict the principles of justice that these real people would choose. This means that he must do without the universalising 'legitimacy' of the *original position* and let *his* views of the principles of justice stand *as his own views*. Rawls can no longer claim the authority of a universal voice.

Nor is Nicola Lacey (1998) necessarily correct in claiming that the 'methodological muddle' of Rawls' concept of the *original position* does not automatically undermine the legitimacy of the emerging principles (p.47). For this methodological muddle is indicative of Rawls' conservative patriarchal elitism. As many critics have pointed out, his choice of the principles of justice simply represents the political *status quo* in the United States, where equal opportunity is nothing more than an empty phrase for those trapped in disadvantage, poverty and powerlessness.

In his 1996 work, *Political Liberalism*, Rawls insists that his critics have mistaken the 'deliberations and motives' of the parties in the *original position* for an account of the moral psychology of real people, when they are 'merely the artificial creatures inhabiting our device of representation' (p.28). But, if these parties are 'merely artificial creatures' then what can they possibly have to do with choosing principles of justice in real societies? And, by what authority does Rawls assume that the *original position* is 'our' (universal) device of representation? He simply continues to assume that his privileged, patriarchal,[12] rationalist world view is *the* world view.

As Moller Okin (1989) points out, while Rawls begins with an acknowledgment of the importance of the family as the major influence on the moral development of future citizens, he then simply assumes that the family as a social institution is essentially just. But, as Moller Okin emphasises, justice within families must be *required* if these institutions are to *be* just and fulfil their responsibility for guiding the moral development of future citizens. Rawls completely ignores the extensive abuse of less powerful members of families, that is, women and children, by male members of those families, as well as the fact that women are socialised to sacrifice their 'fair share' to other family members (pp.22-23,97-99).

However, in his 1999 work, *The Law of Peoples,* where he addresses the issue of international justice, Rawls appears to acknowledge his 'oversight' in leaving women out of his political theory, expressing his gratitude to Susan Moller Okin, and other feminist writers, for pointing this out. And yet, this acknowledgment is cursory in tone, and relegated to a footnote (p.156). It is, in fact, clear from his dismissive discussion of the family, and other private institutions, further on in the same work that Rawls has still not understood the feminists' objections. He makes the remarkable statement that, while political principles of justice do not apply directly to the internal life of the family, they *do* impose essential constraints on family life that *guarantee* the basic rights and liberties of all family members. He then concludes that 'we' would not want political principles of justice to be applied directly to the internal life of the family, and that 'we' must leave non-political, 'private' institutions, such as the family, free from these constraints (p.159).

Nor has Rawls made any significant changes to the other concepts that make up his earlier work. The *original position* remains essentially unchanged, and he continues to champion a 'realistic utopian' view of society, based on an apparently unshakeable faith in reason, despite his acknowledgment of the brutality of human history. While Rawls claims that he is simply hoping for a better future, how can he sustain this hope when his political theory ignores the essential need to constrain oppressive practices in situations where people are powerless and vulnerable?

Judith Shklar (1984,1990) has written passionately and powerfully about the dangers of naïve reliance on rationality in politics. Shklar, a survivor of Nazi Europe, believes that Rawls seriously underestimates the danger and ubiquity of humanity's *illiberal* impulses and the vices inherent in human nature. Rawls appears to be completely oblivious of the need for state protection of individual rights given the 'everyday cruelty' that each citizen encounters, and the fear that this generates.[13]

Communitarianism versus Liberalism

Other commentators have drawn attention to a lack of community values in the Kantian/Rawlsian liberal tradition, where the focus is on individual freedom and rights. Communitarians, such as Michael Sandel (1984) and Alistair MacIntyre (1985),[14] claim that people are essentially social beings and that, therefore, the structure of society is the most appropriate starting point for political theory. Communitarians reject the idea of political theory as an objective search for universal values, claiming that such a theory should be socially grounded and interpretative (Lacey, 1998, p.183). This critique of liberalism is strengthened by the vulnerability of contemporary liberal democracies to the accusation that they simply empower the self-interest of the propertied and elite classes.

And yet, there are significant problems in considering communitarianism as an alternative to liberalism. As Lacey points out, communitarian views have essentially been individual responses to liberalism, rather than contributions to a unified political theory. Also, by giving priority to collective 'community' values, with no allowance for critical review of existing social institutions, communitarians inevitably endorse the *status quo*, compromising the protective rights of community members (pp.183-185). This utopian appeal to 'trust in the collectivity' is a dangerous one given the brutal outcome of the communist regimes of the Twentieth Century.

Levinas: Injustice as the Power of the 'Other'

As Emmanuel Levinas, another survivor of the Nazi horror, points out, justice is no more likely to be found in vague concepts of 'community' than it is in Rawls' impoverished concept of the *original position.* Rather, justice, and injustice, are essential aspects of relating to others and are, therefore, an inescapable part of being (cited in Werhane, 1995, pp.65-66). Justice, and injustice, are the result of power dynamics in social interaction.

This, then, explains the sense of total *dis*empowerment in Levinas' statement that: 'The persecuted one cannot defend himself [*sic*] by language ... Persecution is the precise moment in which the subject is reached or touched without the mediation of the logos.' The persecuted suffer the utmost violence 'of being so very *nothing* for the Other' (cited in Weber, 1995, pp.71-72). Levinas also depicts a familiar ambivalence in our relationship to others,[15] characterised by a self-sacrificing sense of responsibility in constant tension with a hatred of others as potential oppressors (Bernasconi, 1995, pp.77-78).

Contemporary Social Theory: Beyond Rationalist Constraints?

Habermas and Proceduralism

Jurgen Habermas (1984, 1996, 1998) attempts to complete the Kantian/Rawlsian project, and to resolve its problems, in his proceduralist theory of liberal democracy. He proposes a political model based on uncoerced discussion between free and equal individuals attempting to reach a mutually acceptable decision. This is 'the ideal speech situation'. For Habermas, 'communicative power', or 'the consensus-achieving power of communication aimed at mutual understanding', is transformed into 'administrative power' by means of the legal process. He subsequently proposes a 'proceduralist paradigm of law', centred on the procedural conditions of the democratic process, where the places of the 'economic man' [*sic*] or 'welfare-client' are occupied instead by:

> ...a public of citizens who participate in political communication in order to articulate their wants or needs, to give voice to their violated interests, and, above all, to clarify and settle the contested standards and criteria according to which equals are treated equally and unequals unequally ... In place of the zero-sum game between competing initiatives of private and governmental actors, we reckon instead with the complimentary forms of communication found in the private and public spheres of the lifeworld, on the one hand, and in political institutions on the other ... [a legal community] *owes* its legitimacy to the forms of communication in which civic autonomy alone can express and prove itself ... the only solution consists in thematizing the connection between forms of communication that *simultaneously* guarantee private and public autonomy *in the very conditions from which they emerge* (1998, pp.18-19).

But, as William Scheuerman (1999) points out, Habermas offers an ambiguous theory of liberal democracy. While at certain points he appears to be setting the stage for the development of a radical theory, overall, his proposed democratic institutions are incapable of containing powerful markets and administrations (pp.153-156). While Habermas acknowledges that communicative power will need to be better immunised against coercion by 'illegitimate' power (p.19), somehow, he does not quite manage to achieve this. As Michael Rosenfeld (1998) puts it, Habermas' attempt to reconcile democracy, rights and justice places too great a burden on his 'proceduralist paradigm' (pp.111-112).

Habermas needs to go beyond the limits imposed by his proceduralism, and examine the reality of socio-economic inequalities and how these might be remedied, incorporating this analysis into his revised democratic model. Without this crucial step, his concepts of the ideal speech situation, and communicative power, are completely ineffectual as means to promoting participatory democratic debate (Scheuerman, pp.157-166). Axel Honneth (1999) makes the same point when he argues that the ethical norms of social interaction cannot be defined solely in terms of Habermas' rationalist analysis of the linguistic conditions of 'communicative action' as this concept completely ignores the realities of social and political oppression. It seems, therefore, that power differentials remain a shadow in Habermas' work, the implications of which he never quite manages to confront.

Foucault, Power and the 'View from Nowhere'

Michel Foucault (1972, 1993) is generally considered to have dealt with the issue of power more directly than Habermas. Foucault[16] also differs from Habermas in claiming that the Enlightenment obsession with reason has led to the use of knowledge as a weapon of institutional coercion in contemporary western societies. He argues that the Enlightenment's professed noble ideals of human emancipation concealed a Nietzschean 'will to power', developing new 'moral technologies' that resulted in a level of social control far greater than that which existed in traditional societies (cited in Merquior, 1991, p.90).

Foucault also dispenses with the Cartesian idea of 'a grounding subject', viewing ideas in history as discrete forms separate from their psychological and social context (Merquior, pp.17-20). He also made it clear at the outset that his proposed analysis would not address the issue of power at the level of conscious intention. *His* intention was to study power at the point where it becomes completely invested in social practices (Foucault, 1994).

But, despite Foucault's reputation as an innovative thinker, as J. G. Merquior points out, the view that power is ubiquitous to all aspects of life is not an original one (pp.111-113). Nor does this broad assertion contribute to a better understanding of the dangers of power differentials, and how these might be countered. While this is not surprising given Foucault's dismissal of rational critique, the 'knowing' subject, and the interplay of competing interests within society, it is ironic that it also leaves him in a position similar to the rationalist liberals' 'view from nowhere'. So, again, the issue of power has not been directly confronted.

'Difference Feminism' and Power

Difference, or cultural, feminism has become extremely influential at the turn of the century, largely as a result of the views of writers such as Carol Gilligan (1993) and the 'new' French feminists, particularly Luce Irigaray (1993a, 1993b). These authors reject both liberal and radical feminist theories and their strategies for social change, claiming that these approaches are severely limited by their pursuit of equality in terms of the dominant (male) culture. Difference feminists consider this nothing less than a betrayal of 'being a woman'. In their view, sex/gender differences should not be 'glossed over' in an attempt to become one of 'the men's club', but should be celebrated as 'equal but different'.

However, difference feminism does not offer any alternative strategy for dealing with the ongoing oppression of women. Many commentators also point out that this theory not only fails to deal with the problem of oppression, but also unintentionally colludes with the patriarchy by locking women into the inferior role forced upon them by that institution. Earlier feminists have argued that the patriarchy's allocation of 'less valued' character traits to women creates a socially constructed, false, and destructive dichotomy of male and female traits (Lloyd, 1993). It is ironic that difference feminists appear to perpetuate this problem by celebrating these socially constructed 'female' characteristics.

Luce Irigaray's commitment to Lacanian psychoanalysis is also a problem. Lacan's revision of the Freudian phallocentric account of individuation and identity formation perpetuates the familiar patriarchal definitions of the male as powerful and the female as powerless, 'legitimating' the oppression of women. Inevitably, Irigaray's celebration of women as 'equal but different' is vulnerable to suspicions of Lacanian influence (Lacey, pp.207-210).

What is needed is neither a female-centric nor a male-centric view, but an acknowledgment of each person's common humanity and the respect and just treatment that is due to all humans *as humans.* While many feminists, including difference feminists, see this view as inevitably collapsing into the patriarchal definition of human *as male,* this does not necessarily follow if the focus for change remains firmly on achieving a more equitable balance of power. This also expands the discussion to include all who are disadvantaged by power differentials, not only women.

After all, as Nicola Lacey (1998, pp.211ff) points out, Irigaray put aside her usual obscure deconstructionist style, replacing it with a plainly stated appeal to equal protection at law, when addressing specific feminist issues.[17] 'I have regularly worked with women or groups of women who belong to liberation movements, and in these I've observed problems or impasses that can't be resolved except through the establishment of an equitable legal system for both sexes' (cited in Lacey, p.214).

Elements of an Adequate Political Theory

It is interesting to note that Foucault, who built his reputation on the claim that the law, along with all other social and political institutions, is an exclusively coercive agent of disciplinary power (1994b), revised this opinion just before his death. In his last writings,[18] Foucault makes a total conceptual shift:

> The problem is not of trying to dissolve them [relations of power] in the utopia of a perfectly transparent communication, but to give oneself the rules of law, the techniques of management, and also the ethics, the *ethics,* the practices of the self, which would allow these games of power to be played with a minimum of domination (cited in Kelly, 1994, p.391).

An adequate political theory, then, needs to address the centrality of the subject, as well as that subject's interactions with others, and acknowledge that people are not totally rational beings but an amalgam of the rational and non-rational. This, in turn, requires recognition of the central role of power, along with ambivalence toward others, in human interaction. A society which professes a belief in the universal right to individual liberty and self-determination, and that the rule of law should protect this right, must address the problem of power and oppression in social interaction.

As Socrates says to Callicles in Plato's *Gorgias:* '...it's power that leads men to plumb the depths of depravity' (1994, p.133). This, after all, was what led to the development of classical liberalism. That the principle of the universal right to liberty has so often fallen victim to the frailties of the human condition is not a justification for abandoning that principle. Rather, it is a call to pursue this vision even more passionately, no matter how minimal specific achievements might seem.

Notes

1 See Montesquieu (1952); John Locke, (1960); Thomas Paine, (1984); and Immanuel Kant, (1990). I am particularly indebted to the work of Nicola Lacey for providing an informative account of many of the topics discussed in this chapter.

2 In his highly influential essay of 1859, *On Liberty,* John Stuart Mill argued that the only justification for restricting individual liberty is to protect others from harm. However, an acceptable definition of exactly what constitutes harm remains a matter for debate among contemporary liberals (Mill, 1972).

3 Berlin includes such political theorists as Aristotle, Hegel, Marx and Rawls in this tradition. He argues that the rationalist conviction that there is one correct view of the good life easily leads to the justification of abuses of individual rights as a means of bringing the good life to the 'unthinking' masses. For a discussion of this problem with John Rawls' work, as well as the work of other rationalist western writers on political theory, see Judith Shklar (1984, 1990).

4 While Ruth Faden and Tom Beauchamp (1986) do not believe that the concept of informed consent directly confronts issues of social justice, if 'informed consent' involves autonomous action, as well as the making of autonomous choices, as these authors claim, and if socially constructed constraints make both impossible, surely this is unjust.

5 It is also interesting to note that there were 'dreams' at the beginning of the Revolution of a system of free medical care administered by practitioners employed by the state and paid out of the expected income from the sale of church property. These practitioners would be supervised by the state in order to prevent 'abuses'. There were also visions of introducing extensive public health measures, and providing the citizenry with a basic health care education. These 'dreams' did not eventuate (Foucault, 1993, pp.19-20;30-33).

6 This prejudice against women, despite overt claims to belief in liberty for all and the 'rule of reason', is also evident in the writings of Thomas Paine, popular advocate of individual rights and the French and American Revolutions. In his immensely popular work of 1791, *Rights of Man,* Paine is clearly excluding women when he argues that government in a well constituted republic requires 'no belief from any man [*sic*] beyond what his reason can give', and that through this understanding, his human faculties acquire a boldness and a 'gigantic manliness' (Paine, 1984, p.140).

7 And yet, in *On the Relationship of Theory to Practice in Morality in General,* Kant states that everything in morals which is true in theory must also be valid in practice (cited in Reiss, 1991, p.72).

8 The 'democracy' of ancient Greece not only restricted freedom to elite males, but also condoned slavery and the oppression of women (Aristotle, 1985). For Aristotle, a woman's only function was as a means to reproduction: women were instruments for breeding men. Marriage was solely for 'the provision of a stock of the healthiest possible bodies (for) the nurseries of our state.' If it were not for the requirement of reproduction this particular 'deformity in nature (woman)' would never have existed (cited in Susan Moller Okin, 1979, pp.81-83). Aristotle's *Politics* also reveals other remarkable attitudes for a professed rationalist. At one point he states that human nature is driven by greed, therefore the 'inferior' need to be constrained, and their claims for equality and justice ignored. And yet, elsewhere in the same work he claims that reason dominates, along with equality and justice. He then goes on to defend slavery as a legitimate aspect of a free and equal state (1985, pp.41-43;68-69;186;218).

9 Benedict Spinoza, writing in the Seventeenth Century, also attempted to integrate reason and the emotions, doing so in direct response to Rene Descartes argument for the dominance of reason over the 'passions' (cited in Genevieve Lloyd, 1993, p.xiii). Unfortunately for western culture, it was Descartes' view that predominated.

10 Friedrich Nietzsche's view of human nature also contradicted the general homage to rationalism. Along with his belief in the 'will to power', he also claimed that everyone makes judgments that are essentially biased towards their own self-interest, beliefs, values and prejudices, mainly at an unconscious level (Nietzsche, 1990).

11 Male philosophers in western culture have also imposed this false dichotomy upon male and female respectively. Women have consistently been defined as incapable of 'manly' reason and therefore as 'inferior' beings. While this 'double standard' clearly benefits men and oppresses women, many male philosophers have defended this position as 'rational', apparently unaware of the logical incoherence of their arguments. See for example Genevieve Lloyd's discussion of Rousseau, Hegel and Sartre (1993, pp.74-102). Contrary to male beliefs, and despite the formidable obstacles placed in their path, a significant number of women have achieved outstanding intellectual success as philosophers and scientists throughout the past two thousand years (Margaret Alic, 1986; Riane Eisler, 1990; Erica Harth, 1992; and Rosalind Miles, 1989). Given the appalling violence perpetrated almost exclusively by men throughout human history, the following claim by Thomas Aquinas is simply absurd: '...good order would have been wanting in the human family if some [women] were not governed by others wiser than themselves [men] ... because in man, the discretion of reason predominates' (cited in Lloyd, 1993, p.36).

12 For further discussion of this patriarchal bias in Rawls' work see Moira Gatens (1991, pp.67ff). For further discussion of the public/private dichotomy in patriarchal liberal theory see Lacey (1998, pp.71-97).

13 See also Bernard Yack (1996).

14 For an extensive discussion of the limitations of MacIntyre's position see Moller Okin (1986).

15 This is remarkably similar to the Freudian view of the essential ambivalence in human nature: the battle between love and hate for the same Other. And yet, Levinas rejected the psychoanalytic concept of the unconscious aspect of self. But, as William Richardson points out, Levinas' stated denial of the unconscious on the grounds that its existence would place the rational self in jeopardy, carries no real weight. Just because something is difficult to accept does not mean that it does not exist (Richardson, 1995, pp.123-130). See also Llewelyn (1995).

16 See also Michel Foucault (1972, 1993). For a comprehensive overview of Foucault's work see Paul Rabinow (1984). For a comprehensive feminist critique see Lois McNay (1992). And, for a concise overview of contemporary French philosophy see Vincent Descombes (1980).

17 Lacey provides an excellent analysis of the limitations of Irigaray's imaginative and scholarly textual deconstructions in terms of applied feminist issues (pp.211ff).

18 Towards the end of his life, in response to Habermas' objection that if we abandon reason altogether we risk lapsing into irrationality, Foucault conceded that it is equally as dangerous to argue that reason should be totally eliminated, as it is to claim that any criticism of rationality risks a total descent into irrationality (Paul Rabinow, 1984. pp.248-249).

References

Alic, M. (1986), *Hypatia's Heritage: A History of Women in Science from Antiquity to the Late Nineteenth Century*, London: The Women's Press.

Aristotle, *The Politics*, Carnes Lord (trans), (1985), Chicago and London: University of Chicago Press.

Berlin, I. (1969), *Four Essays on Liberty,* London: Oxford University Press.

Bernasconi, R. (1995), ' "Only the Persecuted ... ": Language of the Oppressor, Language of the Oppressed', in A. T. Peperzak, (ed), *Ethics as First Philosophy: The Significance of Emmanuel Levinas for Philosophy, Literature and Religion*, New York and London: Routledge, pp. 77-86.

Boucher, D. and Kelly, P. (eds), (1994), *The Social Contract From Hobbes to Rawls*, London: Routledge.

Descombes, V. (1980), *Modern French Philosophy*, L. Scott-Fox and J. M. Harding (trans), Cambridge: Cambridge University Press.

Eisler, R. (1990), *The Chalice and the Blade: Our History, Our Future*, London: Unwin Paperbacks.

Faden, R. and Beauchamp, T. L. (1986), *A History and Theory of Informed Consent*, New York: Oxford University Press.

Foucault, M. (1972), *The Archaeology of Knowledge*, A. M. Sheridan (trans), London: Tavistock.

Foucault, M. (1993), *The Birth of the Clinic: An Archaeology of Medical Perception*, A. M. Sheridan Smith (trans), London: Tavistock.

Foucault, M. (1994a), 'The Art of Telling the Truth', in M. Kelly (ed), *Critique and Power: Recasting the Foucault/Habermas Debate*, Cambridge, Mass., and London: The MIT Press, pp. 139-148.

Foucault, M. (1994b), 'Two Lectures', in M. Kelly (ed), *Critique and Power: Recasting the Foucault/Habermas Debate*, Cambridge, Mass., and London: The MIT Press, pp. 17-46.

Gatens, M. (1991), *Feminism and Philosophy: Perspectives on Difference and Equality*, Indianapolis: Indiana University Press.

Gay, P. (1994), *The Cultivation of Hatred: The Bourgeois Experience, Victoria to Freud*, Volume 3, London: Harper Collins.

Gilligan, C. (1993), *In a Different Voice: Psychological Theory and Women's Development*, Cambridge: Harvard University Press.

Habermas, J. (1984), *The Theory of Communicative Action*, T. McCarthy (trans), Oxford: Polity Press.

Habermas, J. (1996), *Between Facts and Norms: Contributions to a Discourse Theory of Law and Democracy*, W. Rehg (trans), Cambridge: Polity Press.

Habermas, J. (1998), 'Paradigms of Law', in M. Rosenfeld and A. Arato (eds), *Habermas on Law and Democracy: Critical Exchanges*, Berkeley: University of California Press, pp. 13-25.

Harth, E. (1992), *Cartesian Women: Versions and Subversions of Rational Discourse in the Old Regime*, London: Cornell University Press.

Hindress, B. (1996), *Discourses of Power: From Hobbes to Foucault*, Oxford: Blackwell.

Honneth, A. (1999), 'The Social Dynamics of Disrespect: Situating Critical Social Theory Today', in P. Dews (ed), *Habermas: A Critical Reader*, Oxford: Blackwell, pp. 320-337.

Hume, D. (1971), *A Treatise of Human Nature*, Oxford: Oxford University Press. First published 1740.

Irigaray, L. (1993a), *An Ethics of Sexual Difference*, C. Burke and G. C. Gill (trans), New York: Cornell University Press.

Irigaray, L. (1993b), *Je, Tu, Nous: Toward a Culture of Difference*, A. Martin (trans), New York: Routledge.

Kant, I. (1990), *Foundations of the Metaphysics of Morals and What is Enlightenment?* (2nd ed), L. W. Beck (trans), New York: Macmillan. First published 1784, 1785.

Kelly, M. (1994), 'Foucault, Habermas, and the Self-Referentiality of Critique', in M. Kelly (ed), *Critique and Power: Recasting the Foucault/Habermas Debate*, Cambridge, Mass., and London: MIT Press, pp. 365-400.

Lacey, N. (1998), *Unspeakable Subjects: Feminist Essays in Legal and Social Theory*, Oxford: Hart Publishing.

Llewelyn, J. (1995), *Emmanuel Levinas: The Genealogy of Ethics*, London: Routledge.

Lloyd, G. (1993), *The Man of Reason: 'Male' and 'Female' in Western Philosophy*, (2nd ed), London: Routledge.

Locke, J. (1960), *Two Treatises of Government*, Cambridge: Cambridge University Press. First published 1690.

MacIntyre, A. (1985), *After Virtue: A Study in Moral Theory*, (2nd ed), London: Duckworth.

McNay, L. (1992), *Foucault and Feminism: Power, Gender and the Self*, Cambridge: Polity Press.

Miles, R. (1989), *The Women's History of the World*, London: Paladin.

Merquior, J. G. (1991), *Foucault*, London: Fontana Press.

Mill, J. S. (1972), 'On Liberty', in H. B. Acton (ed), *John Stuart Mill: Utilitarianism, Liberty, Representative Government*, London: J. M. Dent & Sons, pp. 63-120. First published 1859.

Moller Okin, S. (1979), *Women in Western Political Thought*, London: Virago.

Moller Okin, S. (1989), *Justice, Gender and the Family*, New York: Basic Books.

Montesquieu, (1952), *The Spirit of Laws*, T. Nugent (trans), Chicago, London and Toronto: Encyclopedia Britannica. First published 1748.

Nagel, T. (1991), *Equality and Partiality*, New York: Oxford University Press.

Nietzsche, F. (1990), *Beyond Good and Evil*, R. J. Hollingdale (trans), London: Penguin Books.

Nozick, R. (1974), *Anarchy, State and Utopia*, Oxford: Blackwell.

Paine, T. (1984), *Rights of Man*, Harmondsworth: Penguin Books. First published 1791.

Plato (1994), *Gorgias,* R. Waterfield (trans), Oxford: Oxford University Press.

Rabinow, P. (ed), (1984), *The Foucault Reader*, New York: Pantheon Books.

Rawls, J. (1971), *A Theory of Justice*, Oxford: Oxford University Press.

Rawls, J. (1996), *Political Liberalism*, New York: Columbia University Press.

Rawls, J. (1999), *The Law of Peoples*, Cambridge, Mass: Harvard University Press.

Reiss, H. (ed), (1991), *Kant: Political Writings*, H. B. Nisbet (trans), (2nd ed), Cambridge: Cambridge University Press.

Richardson, W. J. (1995), 'The Irresponsible Subject', in A. T. Peperzak, (ed), *Ethics as First Philosophy: The Significance of Emmanuel Levinas for Philosophy, Literature and Religion*, New York and London: Routledge, pp. 123-131.

Rosenfeld, M. (1998), 'Can Rights, Democracy, and Justice Be Reconciled Through Discourse Theory? Reflections on Habermas's Proceduralist Paradigm of Law', in M. Rosenfeld and A. Arato (eds), *Habermas on Law and Democracy: Critical Exchanges*, Berkeley: University of California Press, pp. 82-112.

Sandel, M. (1984), 'Justice and the Good', in M. Sandel (ed), *Liberalism and its Critics*, Oxford: Blackwell.

Schaeffer, D. (1979), *Justice or Tyranny? A Critique of John Rawls's Theory of Justice*, London: Kennicat Press.

Schama, S. (1989), *Citizens: A Chronicle of the French Revolution*, London: Penguin Books.

Scheuerman, W. E. (1999), 'Between Radicialism and Resignation: Democratic Theory in Habermas's *Between Facts and Norms*', in P. Dews (ed), *Habermas: A Critical Reader*, Oxford: Blackwell, pp. 153-177.

Shklar, J. (1984), *Ordinary Vices*, Cambridge, Mass: Harvard University Press.

Shklar, J. (1990), *The Faces of Injustice*, New Haven: Yale University Press.

Weber, E. (1995), 'The Notion of Persecution in Levinas's *Otherwise than Being or Beyond Essence*', in A. T. Peperzak, (ed), *Ethics as First Philosophy: The Significance of Emmanuel Levinas for Philosophy, Literature and Religion*, New York and London: Routledge, pp. 69-76.

Werhane, P. H. (1995), 'Levinas's Ethics: A Normative Perspective without Metaethical Constraints', in A. T. Peperzak, (ed), *Ethics as First Philosophy: The Significance of Emmanuel Levinas for Philosophy, Literature and Religion*, New York and London: Routledge, pp. 59-67.

Yack, B. (ed), (1996), *Liberalism Without Illusions: Essays on Liberal Theory and the Political Vision of Judith N. Shklar*, Chicago: University of Chicago Press.

6 Beyond Legalism: A Feminist Jurisprudence as a Guide to Law Reform?

Introduction

Legal positivism is the dominant legal theory in English speaking common law jurisdictions. For legal positivists, law is rational, impartial and completely separate from questions of morality. The natural law theorist, traditional enemy of the legal positivist, defines law in terms of objective principles of morality evident on rational reflection. However, Judith Shklar (1964) sees this debate as nothing more than a 'family quarrel', given that both theories claim that fixed legal 'rules' are universal and that adjudication is the rational and impartial application of these rules.

The American legal realists of the 1930s were the first to formally criticise the conservative aspects of legalism.[1] However, it was not until the 1970s that the critical legal studies movement evolved, calling for major changes to a legal system seen to be protecting power and privilege behind a façade of professed impartiality. Roberto Unger, whose early work was the inspiration for this movement, proposes a radical vision of law in an 'emancipatory democracy', although protective rights are deeply compromised by his view of the ideal community.

It is Catharine MacKinnon, feminist legal commentator, who directly confronts the issue of law as power. It is this approach to both jurisprudence and law reform that has the most potential for changing unjust power differentials, not only for women, but for all disempowered people in liberal democratic societies.

Legalism and Adjudication: Another Rationalist Illusion

Legal positivists claim that laws set standards that are applied impartially to formally equal parties, and that law is an independent practice, completely separate from politics, ethics and religion. However, these legal theorists have difficulty providing an adequate account of the boundaries between the legal and the non-legal, the source of legal authority, the relationship between law and justice, and the legitimacy of their claim to a distinct, unified body of objective knowledge. Nor can they account for the influence of individual values and beliefs on judicial decision making (Lacey, 1998, pp.5-12).

The Separation of Law and Morals

H. L. A. Hart (1958), the most prominent contemporary legal positivist, insists on the separation of law 'as it is' and law 'as it ought to be'. He turns to Bentham, Nineteenth Century legal positivist, for support, pointing out that Bentham did not deny that legal systems and moral standards influence each other. Nor did he deny that courts might be legally bound to make decisions that are consistent with what they consider to be just. What Bentham *did* claim was that, in the absence of a specific legal provision, the fact that a rule of law violates moral standards does not mean that it is *not* a valid rule of law; nor does the moral desirability of a rule automatically turn it into valid law. Therefore, rules[2] that confer rights need not be moral rules. Hart attempts to justify this claim by using the analogy of 'the rules of a game'. He argues that this is another example of a situation where conferring 'rights' is irrelevant to questions of justice. But, even if this analogy is taken seriously, it does not support Hart's view, for justice as fairness is exactly what the rules of a game *do* embody.

Hart goes on to deny the claim that the legal positivists must at least allow that there is a moral dimension to making judgments about 'hard cases'. While he does acknowledge that the criterion which justifies a decision in such cases is 'some concept of what the law ought to be', he does not accept that such a decision necessarily involves a *moral* dimension. This is to misunderstand the meaning of the word 'ought', which, according to Hart, merely reflects the presence of *some* standard of criticism, which may or may not also be a moral standard. 'Ought' might simply indicate that a particular policy is to be supported, without necessarily endorsing the moral status of that policy, or the moral status of the decision to support it (pp.607-613). After all, Hart concludes, if all standards *were* moral standards, then all legal questions, and rules, would be open to ongoing revision in response to changes in social policy.

However, Hart is not justified in dismissing this conclusion simply because he finds it inconvenient for his point of view. Nor is he correct about the meaning of the word 'ought' in the context in which he uses it. He claims that this word, in this context, simply reflects the presence of some standard of criticism, and does not necessarily refer to morals. However, all 'standards of criticism' *do* necessarily involve a value judgment of some kind, either 'good' or 'bad', and value judgments are moral judgments. Hart insists that any judgment as to whether a law is 'good' or 'bad' is completely separate from 'law as law'; Nazi law was 'bad law' and law in liberal Nineteenth Century England was 'good law' (pp.615-618). But, law *is* inherently value-laden, and a judgment as to whether it is 'good' or 'bad' is part of a continuous moral dimension that begins with the particular values underlying that rule. These are then 'filtered' through the value system of the person making the judgment. Therefore, *values of some kind* are intrinsic to what law *is*, as well as to the interpretation of that law.

Ironically, this view seems to be supported by Bentham's opinion of the shortcomings of the common law, which he considered serious enough to require the replacement of 'judge made law' with a civil code. In his view, common law jurisprudence was inaccessible and illogical, easily manipulated by corrupt judges and plagued by incoherence, while the doctrine of precedent perpetuated unjust decisions. For Bentham, the common law was neither rational nor 'based on immemorial wisdom', as claimed by earlier, classical jurists. It was, instead, a 'shapeless heap of odds and ends', a 'prodigious mass of rubbish'. Judicial decision making was nothing more than an arbitrary process heavily influenced by personal, moral or political 'whims' (Davies, 1994, pp.49-50). As the English common law tradition continues to form the core of the legal system in the jurisdictions under review, and as many of these problems still exist, this description of law as intertwined with judicial values presents a major challenge for contemporary legal positivists like Hart.

Legalistic and Non-legalistic Values

Judith Shklar (1994), in her unique version of liberalism referred to in the previous chapter, is highly critical of rationalist legalism. For Shklar, legal positivism is hopelessly obsessed with the 'proper' liberal spheres of public and private life. It is this obsession, with its unrealistic standards of intellectual objectivity, that prevents these theorists from recognising the extent to which their personal values influence their conceptions of law and morals.

Traditional liberalism is locked into identifying itself with the ideal of a strong but neutral state standing apart from ideological conflicts and, therefore, apart from morality. As the task of law is to preserve order amongst ideological conflicts, it must be free from all that is subjective, contingent, or ideological. But, as Shklar points out, the sheer irrelevance of this view to the real world of law and politics is the price that legal positivists must pay for their grossly over-simplified definition of law.

For Shklar, there are simply legalistic and non-legalistic values. Having to choose between conflicting obligations is not only the most common problem of moral life, but also of adjudication. Both moral and legal decision making involve subjective evaluations and interpretations. While there is less standardisation and institutionalisation in the case of non-legalistic values, the decision making process is fundamentally the same as that of making a judgment at law. Therefore, law and morals should not be classified as separate entities, but regarded as a continuum.

As for the natural law theorists, Shklar believes that their rigid classification of the connection between morality and law, and their insistence on the need for agreement, simply results in another version of legalism. Therefore, she sees the traditional argument between legal positivists and natural law theorists as essentially 'a family quarrel' (pp.58-63).

Surprisingly, this 'family tensions' view appears to be shared by Hart. During his lengthy debate with Patrick Devlin in the 1960s about whether the law should enforce 'private' morality,[3] Hart makes the following comment on the 'analytical or definitional' relationship between law and morals:

> Must some reference to morality enter into an adequate definition of law or legal system? Or is it just a contingent fact that law and morals often overlap (as in their common proscription of certain forms of violence and dishonesty) and that they share a common vocabulary of rights, obligations, and duties? These are famous questions in the long history of the philosophy of law, but perhaps they are not so important as the amount of time and ink expended upon them suggests. Two things have conspired to make discussion of them interminable or seemingly so. The first is that the issue has been clouded by use of grand but vague words like "Positivism" and "Natural Law". Banners have been waved and parties formed in a loud but often confused debate (Hart, 1963, p.2).

But what, then, is justice? For, presumably, this is the central issue for any legal theory. Hart considers it 'the most legal of virtues', and Shklar (1964) agrees. According to Cicero, justice is a personal attribute, implying a sense of fairness and a disposition to award each their due. For legalistic ethics it is the epitome of morality. To adjudicate between competing views as to 'who merits what' is the essence of both ethical and political dispute resolution. For Shklar, more elaborate definitions of justice are unhelpful in that they inevitably obscure its essential nature (pp.108-116).

People call for justice not only when they want the existing rules changed, but also when they want the existing system of rules applied more rigorously, or over a wider area of social conduct. But, how can citizens pursue justice if they are unable to even stake a claim? Ideally, Shklar sees law as central to the democratic process, facilitating just settlement of conflicts in terms of rules sanctioned by the community (pp.143-144). Unfortunately, Shklar has no suggestions as to how this might be made a reality.

Critical Legal Studies, Roberto Unger and the 'Fundamental Contradiction'

The critical legal studies movement in the United States, beginning in the 1970s, directly confronted liberal legalism, hoping not only to disturb the *status quo*, but also to overthrow it. This radical critique has had a major influence on contemporary progressive thinking about legal theory and process. Critical legal theorists argue that everything is contingent, with all human actions acquiring meaning from their specific context. This context dependence, in turn, presents a serious challenge for liberal legalism's idea of 'formal equality', which considers all individuals equal, having abstracted them from their highly *un*equal life contexts. 'Objective' rules are then applied to the process of adjudication. Consequently, 'formal equality' simply reinforces and exacerbates existing inequalities (Greschner, 1987).

Critical legal theorists also object to the liberal claim that legal rules created in the political context are 'arbitrary', while judicial decision making is 'rational and objective'. For critical legal theorists there is no difference between legal reasoning and political argument; both are heavily influenced by ideology and the exercise of power. Law *is* politics. According to this critique, the myth that legal reasoning is separate from political argument is promoted in order to 'legitimate' the exercise of *illegitimate* power, and so to discourage any serious lobbying for significant changes to the existing political and legal systems (Greschner, 1987).

Unger's Emancipatory Democracy

Roberto Unger's early work was the main inspiration for the critical legal studies movement, and he remains the most significant spokesperson for the communitarian left.[4] For Unger (1996), the democratic project is the most powerful set of social ideas in modern history. Ideally, this project involves the identification of areas of 'potential overlap' between the conditions of material progress and those of emancipation of the individual. In order to identify these areas of 'potential overlap' the community needs to experiment with a variety of social practices, supported by the law (pp.28-29). However, as Unger points out, current mainstream legal theory actively restricts this project, denying the conflictual nature of the legal process and the creative potential of this conflict (1986, pp.8-9,18-20).

Central to Unger's vision, therefore, is a radically different legal process. This would include a deeper involvement in assessing the social context of problems that come before the law. For example, a court might decide to intervene in a school, a prison or a voting district, in order to bring about necessary reform (1996, pp.31,180-181). Clearly, this more complex enforcement role would require the judiciary to develop a method of analogical reasoning that allows for the recognition of the conflictual context within which a particular statute or precedent originated, as well as the assumptions, values and beliefs on which it is based. Unger believes that a new branch of government would be needed to support this expanded judicial role, providing extensive investigative, technical, financial and administrative resources (1986, pp.8-20).

Unger also proposes four categories of democratic rights. The first is 'community rights', which would establish an individual's claim to security against the state, organisations and other people.[5] Next, 'immunity rights' in an empowered democracy would include the elimination of certain current guarantees of security, such as consolidated property, which promote exploitation of the less powerful. 'Destabilisation rights' would enforce claims to disrupt social practices that reinforce social hierarchy, division and oppression. And, lastly, 'market rights' would represent claims to a more equitable division of material and social resources (1986, pp.38-39).

This system of rights is designed to support Unger's vision of the ideal community, typified by 'heightened experimentalism', where people would be free to fully participate in communal life according to their preferred 'social arrangements'. Civil society would, of course, need to be reorganised in a way that protected all community groups from oppression by others, although Unger is optimistic that as people are freed from existing structures of social oppression, they would become less dependent, more assertive, and less aggressive. They would no longer be 'the hapless creatures of a destiny imposed by class and culture' (1996, pp.150-157,184-185).

Protective Rights versus the Ideal Community

This final claim, however, is surprising, given that the Marxist view of human nature was thoroughly discredited in the Twentieth Century. Human societies have generally been brutally oppressive structures throughout human history. Humans create societies according to their inherent nature, and will go on doing so regardless of utopian visions that deny the realities of the human condition. It is therefore necessary to begin by accepting this reality, and then making a commitment to work within these constraints with the hope of promoting a more equitable distribution of power, however marginal specific achievements might seem.

After all, this view is consistent with Unger's own concept of the 'Fundamental Contradiction', according to which there is an unavoidable ambivalence between Self and Other in human nature. The Other is simultaneously necessary for freeing the Self, and a threat to the destruction of the Self (cited in Greschner, 1987). Given that the 'Fundamental Contradiction' has been a core concept of his work, and has also been extremely influential among critical legal theorists (Kennedy, 1979), Unger's major conceptual shift towards a more optimistic view of human nature requires a detailed supportive argument, which he does not provide.

A related problem for Unger is that he is left with a major tension between individual rights and the ideal community. While his system of rights is initially justified as necessary for the protection of individual freedom, these rights later take on the role of 'protecting' people from the 'threatening' aspect of experimenting with different ways of community living. Rights are now the means of promoting the 'child's' willingness to risk self-transformation, with Unger calling for a renunciation of the 'illusion' of protective rights (Unger, 1996, pp.166-168). And yet, this view of rights is highly elitist and thoroughly *un*democratic. Unger is now claiming to 'know what is good for the masses'. This is nothing less than sowing the seeds of totalitarianism.

There is also a problem with Unger's view of what he calls 'pessimistic progressive legal reformism'. While he acknowledges that change would need to be incremental, he insists that progressive reformism is too conservative as a strategy for social change. The progressive reformists' attempts to maximise access to protective rights within the constraints imposed by the established institutional order are unacceptable to Unger, who sees this as simply reinforcing the authority of the existing social structure (1996, pp.81,96-97).

And yet, how can Unger justify giving priority to a dream, while there is a real need to protect individual rights *now*? Surely this is a dangerous view, setting the stage for continued oppression, rather than its containment. As Donna Greschner (1987) points out, a 'revolution' occurs whenever the lives of ordinary people are changed for the better, even if these changes are inevitably modest. In my view, *this* is visionary.

Beyond Legalism: A Feminist Jurisprudence as a Guide to Effective Law Reform?

While feminist legal commentators of the 1980s and 1990s generally condemned the critical legal studies movement for not going beyond textual 'deconstruction' (Lacey, 1998; Bartlett and Kennedy, 1991), many contemporary feminists are now abandoning progressive reformism in response to the limited success of recent feminist law reform programs. Some feminists are involved in an anxious search for alternative change strategies (Smart, 1989), while others appear to have retreated to the comfort zone of difference, or cultural, feminism. There are also those who view this patriarchal 'backlash' as a 'call' for renewed efforts at law reform.

Feminist Law Reform and Patriarchal 'Backlash'

As Katharine Bartlett and Rosanne Kennedy (1991) point out, the legal doctrine of precedent results in a common law system that is essentially resistant to change. Therefore, pursuing equality by means of law reform in an essentially unequal society can seem overwhelmingly self-defeating. Feminist law reform programs have often provoked a reassertion of patriarchal power, with 'winning' resulting in an even more oppressive patriarchal 'backlash'. Nor is this surprising, given that the purpose of the English common law system, formally established in the Twelfth Century, is essentially to preserve stability and the existing hierarchical structure. Nevertheless, Bartlett and Kennedy conclude that it is essential to remember that *law is power*. Therefore, while law reform may create a patriarchal 'backlash', and its positive effects may be modest, it remains a necessary precondition for meaningful social change (pp.2-11).

Catharine MacKinnon (1991a) has focused directly on this issue of power, cutting through the constraints of the 'difference' and 'equality' approaches to feminist legal reform. As MacKinnon makes clear, the way that women reason morally is not morality in a different voice, a caring voice, as claimed by contemporary difference, or cultural, feminists. It is simply the 'feminine' voice, a voice that has been completely moulded by men to meet their needs. The *powerless* do not have a voice of their own. The 'difference' approach, therefore, effectively reinforces male supremacy and the *status quo*.

According to MacKinnon, the 'equality' approach also fails to present a direct challenge to the inequitable distribution of power, a problem prior to that of gender. MacKinnon's project is jurisprudential, aiming to expose the oppressive aspects of mainstream jurisprudence, and to change the balance of power. From this point of view, power abuse comes before 'difference', whether it involves gender, race, indigenous peoples, class, wealth, education, or any other perceived 'difference'. MacKinnon's goal is to access a fair share of power: 'Take your foot off our necks' and then it might be possible to hear women's voices (pp.89-91).

However, Carol Smart (1989) is concerned that a feminist jurisprudence will simply end up being engulfed by the positivistic tradition of patriarchal law. Smart believes that feminism should, instead, turn to a deconstruction of the gender biased nature of law, aiming to 'decentre' that law. But, even so, Smart concedes that law remains an important strategic element in political confrontations; she would not want to return to a time when women had no legal entitlements (pp.69-71,88-89). Smart is certainly not willing to give up the right to a legal identity, to citizenship, to own property, to earn a living, to initiate divorce, to obtain an education and to enter 'the professions'. Overall, Smart seems undecided as to exactly what her recommendations are for social and political change.

Feminist Jurisprudence and Power

The power of law cannot be overestimated. In Eighteenth Century England William Blackstone, revered by the patriarchy as one of the most eminent jurists in common law history, codified laws that defined women as *femmes covertes*, that is, 'hidden' within the husband or male relatives domestic 'realm'. At law, women had no individual legal identity. Daughters and wives could be sold in the common marketplace as legally owned property. Any property a woman brought to a marriage, and any money made during the marriage, automatically belonged to the husband (Scutt and Graham, 1984). Throughout medieval Europe the law condoned the murder of an adulterous wife by her husband, as well as the 'right' of the husband to inflict corporal punishment as he wished (O'Faolin and Martines, 1979). In England, in 1856, Mary Anne Thomson was sold by her husband for 20 shillings and a dog. 'Gentleman, I have to offer to your notice my wife ... whom I mean to sell to the highest and fairest bidder ... may God deliver us from troublesome wives ... avoid them as you would a mad dog' (Scutt and Graham, 1984, pp.87-88).

There are also many other examples of the legal sanctification of oppression and abuse, involving indigenous peoples, those living in poverty, minority groups and others disempowered by the social hierarchy. Smart is undoubtedly right in not wanting to give up those emancipatory law reforms fought for by early liberal feminists, but she is not right in wanting to give up the contemporary law reform project. On the contrary, history points to the need for a renewed effort, with a model of jurisprudence that recognises power abuse as the core problem of oppression and inequality.

Universal Rights and the Common Law: Irreconcilable Differences?

As demonstrated earlier, the right to informed choice of medical services continues to fall victim to a judicial preoccupation with conservative social and political values, resulting in the protection of the interests of powerful, highly educated, upper class, white males. The *status quo* is jealously guarded, either consciously or unconsciously. Consider the case law once again.

In the 1985 English case, *Sidaway v Bethlem Royal Hospital Governors and Others*,[6] as already noted, the plaintiff suffered nerve root and spinal cord damage following spinal surgery. These were known risks about which she had not been warned. However, the majority of expert evidence supported the non-disclosure of risks in this instance as responsible medical practice. The plaintiff was unsuccessful. And yet, Lord Diplock stated that:

> But, when it comes to warning about risks, the kind of training and experience that a judge will have undergone at the Bar makes it natural for him to say (correctly) it is my right to decide whether any particular thing is done to my body, and I want to be fully informed of any risks there may be involved of which I am not already aware from my general knowledge as a highly educated man of experience, so that I may form my own judgement [*sic*] whether to refuse the advised treatment or not (at 659).

There could hardly be a clearer statement that 'rights' are for the privileged elite, but not for the 'ordinary' person.

And, again, in the 1985 Australian case *Gover v State of South Australia and Perriam*[7] the defendant medical practitioner was held not to have been negligent for failing to advise of the risk of possible blindness associated with surgery to the upper eyelids. The court concluded that the risk of blindness in this situation had not entered the general body of relevant professional knowledge at the time the procedure was carried out in February 1979, and therefore the defendant could not reasonably be expected to have been aware of this risk. Justice Cox stated that:

> I think that the community, and the law, are entitled to expect that an eye surgeon will find some way of informing himself [*sic*] promptly of such an important discovery as a causal relationship between the kind of operation he regularly performs and such a drastic complication as blindness. He must keep up with his reading and know what is being published by researchers in his

> field ... A man is not necessarily negligent because he does not read every new publication that happens to be available, even the latest edition of a well-known text book. I accept Dr Perriam's evidence that he was not aware in February 1979 of a real risk of blindness for an upper lid blepharoplasty. Given that he was a teacher as well as a practicing surgeon, this is perhaps surprising ... I do not think ... that I should find that a competent Adelaide eye surgeon should have realised in February 1979 that blindness was a possible complication in the performance of an upper lid blepharoplasty (at 562).

This conclusion is puzzling. The court was aware that at the time of the surgery, in February 1979, there had been several references to this complication following upper lid blepharoplasty. There had been an article in the *Medical Journal of Australia* in 1973 and an account in a 1976 edition of a standard ophthalmology textbook. There were also other articles referring to this complication in 1973, 1978 and 1979, after which the problem was, according to expert medical witnesses in the case, generally recognised by the medical community (at 561). But, if knowledge of this risk was published in a standard textbook on the subject of the defendant's specialty three years prior to the surgery in question, how can this information not be considered general knowledge in that specialty? Surely an eye surgeon who is both practicing and teaching should be aware of information contained in a current edition of a standard textbook on that specialty. Once again, the interests of the educated, patriarchal elite are preserved, perhaps unconsciously, at the expense of the plaintiff.

The Tort of Negligence and Protective Rights

Marjorie Schultz (1995) suggests that the vulnerability of plaintiffs' interests in relation to the tort of negligence could be remedied by recognising the right to self-determination as a distinct legal interest in *medical choice*. This would require the development of a new legal model within the tort law system that ensures an equitable division of authority between client and medical practitioner (pp.276-299). Joseph Goldstein (1975) expressed a similar view 20 years earlier, arguing that the law should recognise that a person can be wronged without being physically harmed. He believes that a person's dignity as a human being has been violated, and an assault taken place, the moment a medical practitioner commences treatment without have disclosed the relevant information, even if this treatment turns out to have beneficial effects. For Goldstein, the issue should be one of self-determined choice, not consent (p.691).

But, is this simply expecting too much of tort law? There is, after all, no agreement among legal scholars as to whether or not tort law is based on any specific principles. While tort law scholarship emerged in the 1960s with commentators defining its purpose in terms of economic efficiency, that is, awarding monetary compensation for harm done, in the 1970s other legal scholars argued that its foundations rested on moral grounds. Some have even claimed that tort law cannot be explained in terms of a single principle or value, and that it is based on a number of different norms (Owen, 1995, pp.2,13).

The difficulty here is that if there are no clear principles underlying tort law, how is it possible for it to protect individual rights? Contemporary common law in the jurisdictions under review still reflects its origins in English classical common law theory of the Sixteenth to Eighteenth Centuries. Common, or customary, law was thought to be the result of accumulated communal wisdom, distinct from, and superior to, statutes created by politically motivated legislatures or monarchs. Judges did not exercise their *personal* judgment in determining the correct principle of law to apply to a particular case. The only test of a maxim as a rule of common law was that it had 'always been the custom to observe it' (Davies, 1994, pp.24-27).

This, of course, results in an extremely conservative body of law, resistant to change and development. It also results in a body of law that represents social 'custom' according to the beliefs of the privileged elite, with a judiciary generally identifying with those in power. Blackstone, as already noted, was centrally involved in the codification of the non-legal status of women, and Hale, another jurist revered by patriarchal law, produced 'brilliant' legal justifications for the persecution of witches. Nor did classical common law theory include any concept of universal individual human rights, which is not surprising given that this idea did not become an integral part of progressive western thought until the end of the Eighteenth Century.[8]

Traditional legalists are quick to condemn the occasional progressive member of the judiciary for making changes to the common law which clearly break with custom and precedent. However, in making the 'accusation' of failing to follow the dictates of legalism, these traditionalists assume that it is only the decisions of progressive judges that reflect personal values and beliefs; and that those who remain faithful to legalism are unquestionably objective and impartial. But, this is to misunderstand traditionalist, legalistic decision making, which, because it reflects and reinforces the conservative bias of the majority of the judiciary, is generally consistent with custom and precedent. This decision making process is no different from that of the progressive judiciary in that it is also influenced by personal values and beliefs.

This lack of insight on the part of the traditionalist is evident in the comments made by the Chief Justice of Australia, Murray Gleeson, in New

York on 4 July 2000. Gleeson was adamant that judges who disagree with certain laws should either 'put up with them' or resign. Gleeson believes that to be judicial is to be impartial. Judges must apply legal method, and not their personal values, to their work. To use judicial authority on behalf of a cause is to risk 'undermining the foundation upon which such authority rests'. As a legal conservative, Gleeson rejects the 'creative' decision making of the Australian High Court under his more progressive predecessor, former Chief Justice Anthony Mason.[9]

The comments of the Australian High Court in *Breen v Williams*[10] in 1996, where the Court held that Australians do not have a legal right of access to their medical records in the private medical sector, are also revealing. Justices Dawson and Toohey made the following comment on the role of precedent:

> Any changes in legal doctrine, brought about by judicial creativity, must "fit" within the body of rules and principles. The judges of Australia cannot, so to speak, "make it up" as they go along. It is a serious constitutional mistake to think that the common law courts have authority to "provide a solvent" for every social, political or economic problem ... In a democratic society, changes in the law that cannot logically or analogically be related to existing common law rules and principles are the province of the legislature (at 290).

The right to self-determination, to access a fair share of the power needed to maximise life choices, and the right not to be oppressed by others, are all basic human rights due to all by virtue of their humanity. It is a matter of mutual obligation within the human family that each respect the rights of others, as well as claiming them on their own behalf. However, the flawed nature of the human condition, and the resultant violation of the rights of others, whether consciously or unconsciously, makes it essential to constrain those in positions of power. This constraint can only be effective under law that is comprehensive and enforceable. After all, this is the professed goal of the liberal rule of law, and it is up to both governments and citizenry to make sure that it is not abandoned to manipulation by the powerful, at the expense of everyone else. With a common law heritage that protects the interests of power and privilege there is an urgent need for unambiguous and enforceable legislation that will protect the right of every citizen to informed and voluntary choice of medical services.

Notes

1 According to Judith Shklar, the American Legal Realists did not seriously question legalistic morals and politics; their aim was limited to incorporating new 'legal experts'

into the process in order to promote greater order in public life. Shklar believes that legal realism became just as rule-bound as traditional legalism (1964, pp.96, 98).

2 Primary legal rules grant rights or impose obligations on community members. Secondary rules stipulate how and by whom such primary rules may be formed, recognised, modified or extinguished. Rules may be binding because they are either *accepted* or *valid.* Valid rules are those that are binding because they have been treated according to the stipulations of a secondary rule. Hart calls a secondary rule a 'rule of recognition', giving the United States Constitution as an example. Ronald Dworkin (1978, 1986), a liberal whose work faces much the same constraints as that of John Rawls, has argued extensively and stolidly against the positivist distinction between law and morals. However, it is interesting to note that his argument, that is, that all judicial discretion involves reference to 'settled' moral principles, leaves him far more constrained by legalism than the legal positivist.

3 This debate took place in England in the 1960s in response to the *Wolfenden Report: Report of the Committee on Homosexual Offences and Prostitution,* 1957. The brief of this Committee was to decide upon the extent to which the English criminal law should enforce morality, with particular reference to homosexual acts between consenting adults conducted in private and prostitution conducted in private. The Committee decided that it is not the function of the law to intervene in the private lives of citizens, or to enforce any particular patterns of behaviour, apart from those involving the preservation of public order and decency, and the protection of citizens from that which is offensive or harmful, exploitative or corrupting. The Committee's view was that neither homosexuality nor prostitution, as long as the relevant acts took place in private, were the 'business' of the criminal law (Mitchell, 1970, pp.1-3). Patrick Devlin (1965) objected strongly to the Committee's decision, arguing that it is the role of the law to enforce the morality of the 'man on the bus' in order to preserve the social 'fabric'. Hart, not surprisingly, took the opposite view, supporting the individual citizen's right to act as they choose, referring to J. S. Mill's celebrated argument for the claim that the only justification for state intervention to curtail individual freedom is to prevent harm to others. For detailed commentary on this debate see Mitchell (1970) and Wasserstrom (1971).

4 According to Unger (1996), rationalising legal analysis is the retrospective and rationalistic reconstruction of legal decisions in the language of idealised policy and principle. Rationalising legal analysis denies the disorder, conflict and compromise that is an inevitable part of the legal process, in an apparent attempt to prevent arbitrariness in legal decision making. However, by reconstructing large sections of law in order to impose an artificially rational pattern on the total body of law, rationalising legal analysis imposes its own arbitrariness on legal decision making (pp.53-55,64-67).

5 The legal entitlements of communal life would legally enforce many of the expectations involved in relationships of mutual reliance and vulnerability not currently dealt with by the law. This would incorporate standards of good faith, loyalty and responsibility. The right holders themselves, or, if they fail, the judiciary, would set the boundaries to the exercise of these rights according to the effect that the proposed exercise of a right seems likely to have upon the parties to the relationship (1986, pp.38-39).

6 [1985] 1 AC 871; 1 All ER 643 (HL).

7 *Gover v State of South Australia and Perriam* (1985) 39 SASR 543.

8 For a concise account of the development of the concept of universal individual rights, or human rights, and the relationship of this concept to contemporary law see Kinley (1998) and O'Neill and Handley (1994).

9 *The Australian*, 4 July 2000.

10 *Breen v Williams* (1996) 138 ALR 259.

References

Bartlett, K. T. and Kennedy, R. (1991), 'Introduction', in K. T. Bartlett and R. Kennedy (eds), *Feminist Legal Theory: Readings in Law and Gender*, Boulder: Westview Press, pp.1-12.

Davies, M. (1994), *Asking the Law Question*, Sydney: Law Book Company.

Devlin, P. (1965), *The Enforcement of Morals*, Oxford: Oxford University Press.

Dworkin, R. (1978), *Taking Rights Seriously*, London: Duckworth.

Dworkin, R. (1986), *Law's Empire*, Cambridge, Mass: Belknop Press.

Goldstein, J. (1975), 'For Harold Lasswell: Some Reflections on Human Dignity, Entrapment, Informed Consent, and the Plea Bargain', *The Yale Law Journal*, vol. 84, pp. 683-703.

Greschner, D. (1987), 'Judicial Approaches to Equality and Critical Legal Studies', in S. L. Martin and K. E. Mahoney, (eds), *Equality and Judicial Neutrality*, Toronto: Carswell, pp. 59-70.

Hart, H. L. A. (1958), 'Positivism and the Separation of Law and Morals', *Harvard Law Review*, vol. 71 (4), pp. 593-629.

Hart, H. L. A. (1961), *Concept of Law*, London: Clarendon Press.

Hart, H. L. A. (1963), *Law, Liberty and Morality*, London: Oxford University Press.

Kennedy, D. (1979), 'The Structure of Blackstone's Commentaries', *Buffalo Law Review*, vol. 28, pp.209-382.

Kinley, D. (1998), 'The Legal Dimension of Human Rights', in D. Kinley, (ed), *Human Rights in Australian Law*, Sydney: The Federation Press, pp. 2-25.

Lacey, N. (1998), *Unspeakable Subjects: Feminist Essays in Legal and Social Theory*, Oxford: Hart Publishing.

MacKinnon, C. A. (1991a), 'Difference and Dominance: On Sex Discrimination', in K. T. Bartlett and R. Kennedy, (eds), *Feminist Legal Theory: Readings in Law and Gender*, Boulder: Westview Press, pp. 81-94.

MacKinnon, C. A. (1991b), 'Feminism, Marxism, Method and the State', in K. T. Bartlett and R. Kennedy, (eds), *Feminist Legal Theory: Readings in Law and Gender*, Boulder: Westview Press, pp. 181-200.

Mitchell, B. (1970), *Law, Morality and Religion in a Secular Society*, London: Oxford University Press.

O'Faolin, J. and Martines, L. (eds), (1979), *Not in God's Image: Women in History*, London: Virago.

O'Neill, N. and Handley, R. (1994), *Retreat from Injustice: Human Rights in Australian Law*, Leichhardt, New South Wales: The Federation Press.

Owen, D. G. (1995), 'Why Philosophy Matters to Tort Law', in D. G. Owen, (ed), *Philosophical Foundations of Tort Law*, Oxford: Clarendon Press, pp. 1-27.

Schultz, M. (1995), 'From Informed Consent to Patient Choice: A New Protected Interest', *The Yale Law Journal*, vol. 95 (2), pp. 219-299.

Scutt, J. A. and Graham, D. (1984), *For Richer, For Poorer: Money, Marriage and Property Rights*, Melbourne: Penguin Books.

Shklar, J. N. (1964), *Legalism*, Cambridge, Mass: Harvard University Press.

Smart, C. (1989), *Feminism and the Power of Law*, London: Routledge.

Unger, R. M. (1976, c1975), *Knowledge and Politics*, New York: Free Press.

Unger, R.M. (1986), *The Critical Legal Studies Movement*, Cambridge, Mass: Harvard University Press.
Unger, R. M. (1996), *What Should Legal Analysis Become?* London: Verso.
Unger, R. M. (1997), *Politics: The Central Texts*, Zhiyuan Cui (ed), London and New York: Verso.
Unger, R. M. (1998), *Democracy Realized: The Progressive Alternative*, London and New York: Verso.
Wasserstrom, R. A. (ed), (1971), *Morality and the Law*, Belmont, California: Wadsworth.

Cases

Breen v Williams (1996) 138 ALR 259.
Gover v State of South Australia and Perriam (1985) 39 SASR 543.
Sidaway v Bethlem Royal Hospital Governors and Others [1985] 1 AC 871; 1 All ER 643 (HL).

7 Changing the Balance of Power

Introduction

It is evident from the above discussion that comprehensive statutory regulation of the medical community is essential in order to protect the right of every citizen to informed choice of medical services. Clear and detailed requirements need to be drawn up, meaningful sanctions imposed for violations, and the law strictly enforced. Protection of the rights and safety of health care clients must be given priority, not the preservation of the medical community's power and privileges.

Also, once the right to informed choice is effectively enforced, health care costs to the state should fall significantly. Clinical practices aimed solely at increasing the medical practitioner's income should be significantly curtailed. As these practices are obviously dependent upon overriding the client's right to informed choice, when medical practitioners no longer feel free to ignore this right, there will be little opportunity to indulge in these fraudulent practices.

Enforcement

Comprehensive systems of independent client advocates with statutory authority to monitor compliance at the clinical level, and to act decisively in instances of non-compliance, are urgently needed. Advocates could be allocated to specific health care regions, as an extension of the existing network of health care complaints services. This would mean that those complaints services currently without statutory powers to act as client advocates would become truly effective. While this suggestion is far from new, and incremental advances have been made in some of the jurisdictions under review, in general, health care clients continue to be denied this essential service. It is a poor reflection on liberal democratic societies that state provision of health care advocacy services has to be argued for time and time again.

Those who argue for a conciliatory, as opposed to an adversarial, solution to the problem of *un*informed choice claim that alternative dispute resolution services are preferable to the confrontational nature of legal disputes and other forms of advocacy. However, once again, those who adopt this view overlook the effect of power differentials between disputing parties. If one party possesses considerably more power than the other, then the conflict may very well be promptly resolved, but this will be at the expense of the less powerful party. A mediator is not an advocate and cannot act to remedy power imbalances between disputing parties. The essential point is that an advocate, as opposed to a mediator, acts exclusively on behalf of their client and directly confronts power differentials that disadvantage their client's negotiating capacity.

Additional Change Strategies

Additional change strategies could include public education campaigns detailing the rights of health care clients; education of medical students, *by client representatives*, about these rights; and establishment of tribunals that are completely independent of the medical community. Regular public forums allowing for community debate about the limitations of contemporary medicine, as well as sharing stories of client experience, could also be established. Finally, the medical monopoly of health care policy making bodies should be replaced by a balanced representation of all relevant parties, giving the community a voice in the ongoing review of its health care needs.

Conclusion

While the medical community is no worse, or better, than any other group within the human family, it is arguably one of the most dangerous when 'out of control', precisely because of the unique vulnerability of the person seeking advice about their health care. To ignore the hard lessons of the past, including the importance of containing the destructive instincts in the human psyche, is to unnecessarily perpetuate pain and suffering for those who are vulnerable to rights violations by powerful groups. Even if the community's ability to contain these destructive instincts is relatively limited, as I have argued, it seems to me that every effort made to at least reach this limit holds within it the hope of a better future. I believe that, with an open mind, we *can* learn from the past and work for that better future.

Bibliography

Alic, M. (1986), *Hypatia's Heritage: A History of Women in Science from Antiquity to the Late Nineteenth Century*, London: The Women's Press.

Annas, G. (1984), 'Why the British Courts Rejected the American Doctrine of Informed Consent', *Public Health and the Law*, vol. 74 (11), pp. 1281-1286.

Annas, G. J. (1992), 'The Nuremberg Code in US Courts: Ethics versus Expediency', in G. J. Annas and M. A. Grodin (eds), *The Nazi Doctors and the Nuremberg Code: Human Rights in Human Experimentation*, New York: Oxford University Press, pp. 201-222.

Annas, G. J. (1998), *Some Choice: Law, Medicine, and the Market*, New York: Oxford University Press.

Annas, G. J. and Grodin, M. A. (1992), 'Judgment and Aftermath', in G. J. Annas and M. A. Grodin (eds), *The Nazi Doctors and the Nuremberg Code: Human Rights in Human Experimentation*, New York: Oxford University Press, pp. 94-107.

Aristotle, (1985), *The Politics*, Carnes Lord (trans), Chicago and London: University of Chicago Press.

Australian Department of Human Services and Health, (1993), *The Health/Medical Care Injury Case Study Project: A Research Paper*, Canberra: Australian Government Publishing Service.

Australian Department of Human Services and Health, (1995), *Review of Professional Indemnity Arrangements for Health Care Professionals: Compensation and Professional Indemnity in Health Care*, Final Report, Canberra: Australian Government Publishing Service.

Barker-Benfield, G. J. (1977), 'Sexual Surgery in Late Nineteenth Century America', in C. Dreifus (ed), *Seizing our Bodies: The Politics of Women's Health*, New York: Vintage Books, pp. 13-41.

Bartlett, K. T. and Kennedy, R. (1991), 'Introduction', in K. T. Bartlett and R. Kennedy (eds), *Feminist Legal Theory: Readings in Law and Gender*, Boulder: Westview Press, pp.1-12.

Beauchamp, T. L. and Bowie, N. E. (1997), *Ethical Theory and Business*, (5th ed), New Jersey: Prentice-Hall.

Beauchamp, T. L. and Childress, J. F. (1994), *Principles of Biomedical Ethics*, (4th ed), New York: Oxford University Press.

Beauchamp, T. L. and McCullough, L. B. (1988), 'The Management of Medical Information: Legal and Moral Requirements of Informed Voluntary Consent', in R. Edwards and G. C. Graber, (eds), *Bioethics*, San Diego: Harcourt Brace Jovanovich, pp. 130-141.

Beecher, H. (1966), 'Ethics and Clinical Research', *New England Journal of Medicine*, vol. 274, pp. 1354-1360.

Bender, L. (1988), 'A Lawyer's Primer on Feminist Theory and Tort', *Journal of Legal Education*, vol. 38 (1&2), pp. 3-37.

Benidickson, J. (1995), 'Canadian Developments in Health Care Liability and Compensation', in S. A. M. McLean, (ed), *Law Reform and Medical Injury Litigation*, Aldershot: Dartmouth, pp. 5-30.

Bennet, B. (1997), *Law and Medicine*, Sydney: Law Book Company.

Berlant, J. (1975), *Profession and Monopoly: A Study of Medicine in the United States and Great Britain*, Berkeley: University of California Press.

Berlin, I. (1969), *Four Essays on Liberty*, London: Oxford University Press.

Bernasconi, R. (1995), ' "Only the Persecuted ... ": Language of the Oppressor, Language of the Oppressed', in A. T. Peperzak, (ed), *Ethics as First Philosophy: The Significance of Emmanuel Levinas for Philosophy, Literature and Religion*, New York and London: Routledge, pp. 77-86.

Blustein, J. (1993), 'Doing What the Patient Orders: Maintaining Integrity in the Doctor-Patient Relationship', *Bioethics*, vol. 7 (4), pp. 289-314.

British Medical Association, (1992), *Medicine Betrayed: The Participation of Doctors in Human Rights Abuses*, London: Zed Books.

Boucher, D. and Kelly, P. (eds), (1994), *The Social Contract From Hobbes to Rawls*, London: Routledge.

Brock, D. W. (1991), 'The Ideal of Shared Decision-Making Between Physicians and Patients', *Kennedy Institute of Ethics Journal*, March, pp. 28-47.

Brody, H. (1992), *The Healer's Power*, New Haven: Yale University Press.

Brownmiller, S. (1974), *Against Our Will: Men, Women and Rape*, Harmondsworth: Penguin Books.

Buchanan, A. E. (1996), 'Is There a Medical Profession in the House?' in R. G. Spece, D. S. Shimm and A. E. Buchanan (eds), *Conflicts of Interest in Clinical Practice and Research*, New York: Oxford University Press, pp. 105-136.

Buchanan, A. E. and Brock, D. W. (1990), *Deciding for Others: The Ethics of Surrogate Decision-Making*, Cambridge: Cambridge University Press.

Coady, C. A. J. (1996), 'On Regulating Ethics', in M. Coady and S. Bloch (eds), *Codes of Ethics and the Professions*, Melbourne: Melbourne University Press, pp. 269-287.

Coady, C. A. J. and Sampford, C. J. G. (eds), (1993), *Business, Ethics and the Law*, Sydney: The Federation Press.

Coney, S. and Bunkle, P. (1988), 'An Unfortunate Experiment', *Bioethics News*, vol. 8 (1), pp. 3-31.

Consumers' Health Forum of Australia, (1990), *Legal Recognition and Protection of the Rights of Health Consumers*, Canberra.

Consumers' Health Forum of Australia, (undated), *Consumer Health Rights: A Summary of your Health Rights and Responsibilities*, pamphlet, Canberra.

Daniels, N. (1984), 'Understanding Physician Power', *Philosophy and Public Affairs*, vol. 13 (40), pp. 347-357.

Daniels, N. (1985), *Just Health Care*, Cambridge: Cambridge University Press.

Darvall, L. (1993), *Medicine, Law and Social Change: The Impact of Bioethics, Feminism and Rights Movements on Medical Decision-Making*, Sydney: Dartmouth.

Davies, M. (1994), *Asking the Law Question*, Sydney: Law Book Company.

de Navarre, M. (1984), *The Heptameron*, P. A. Chilton (trans), London: Penguin Books.

Descombes, V. (1980), *Modern French Philosophy*, L. Scott-Fox and J. M. Harding (trans), Cambridge: Cambridge University Press.

de Troyes, C. (1987), *Arthurian Romances*, D. D. R. Owen (trans), London: D. M. Dent & Sons.

Devlin, P. (1965), *The Enforcement of Morals*, Oxford: Oxford University Press.

Douzinous, C. Warrington, R. and McVeigh, S. (1991), *Postmodern Jurisprudence: The Law of Texts in the Texts of Law*, London: Routledge.

Drache, D. and Sullivan, T. (1999), 'Health Reform and Market Talk: Rhetoric and Reality', in D. Drache and T. Sullivan (eds), *Market Limits in Health Reform: Public Success, Private Failure*, London and New York: Routledge, pp. 1-21.

Dunn, I. (1993), 'What should doctor tell you?' *Law Institute Journal*, April, pp. 268-271.

Dworkin, R. (1978), *Taking Rights Seriously*, London: Duckworth.

Dworkin, R. (1986), *Law's Empire*, Cambridge, Mass: Belknop Press.

Eisler, R. (1990), *The Chalice and the Blade: Our History, Our Future*, London: Unwin Paperbacks.

Evans, R. (1996), 'Health Reform: What 'Business' is it of Business?' in D. Drache and T. Sullivan (eds), *Market Limits in Health Reform: Public Success, Private Failure*, London and New York: Routledge, pp. 25-47.

Faden, R. and Beauchamp, T. L. (1986), *A History and Theory of Informed Consent*, New York: Oxford University Press.

Feldberg, G. and Vipod, R. (1999), 'The Virus of Consumerism', in D. Drache and T. Sullivan (eds), *Market Limits and Health Reform: Public Success, Private Failure*, London and New York: Routledge, pp. 48-64.

Fisher, S. (1986), *In the Patient's Best Interest: Women and the Politics of Medical Decisions*, New Brunswick, New Jersey: Rutgers University Press.

Foucault, M. (1972), *The Archaeology of Knowledge*, A. M. Sheridan (trans), London: Tavistock.

Foucault, M. (1993), *The Birth of the Clinic: An Archaeology of Medical Perception*, A. M. Sheridan Smith (trans), London: Tavistock.

Foucault, M. (1994a), 'The Art of Telling the Truth', in M. Kelly (ed), Critique and Power: *Recasting the Foucault/Habermas Debate*, Cambridge, Mass., and London: The MIT Press, pp. 139-148.

Foucault, M. (1994b), 'Two Lectures', in M. Kelly (ed), Critique and Power: *Recasting the Foucault/Habermas Debate*, Cambridge, Mass., and London: The MIT Press, pp. 17-46.

Freckelton, I. (1996), 'Enforcement of Ethics', in M. Coady and S. Bloch (eds), *Codes of Ethics and the Professions*, Melbourne: Melbourne University Press, pp. 130-165.

Freckelton, I. (1999a), 'Doctors as Witnesses', in I. Freckelton and K. Petersen (eds), *Controversies in Health Law*, Sydney: The Federation Press, pp. 86-106.

Freckelton, I. (1999b), 'Malpractice Actions Against Health Care Providers,' in I. Freckelton and K. Petersen (eds), *Controversies in Health Law*, Sydney: The Federation Press, pp. 107-133.

Freidson, E. (1970), *Profession of Medicine: A Study of the Sociology of Applied Knowledge*, New York: Harper & Row.

Freidson, E. (1975), *Doctoring Together: A Study of Professional Social Control*, New York: Elsevier Scientific Publishing.

French, M. (1985), *Beyond Power: On Women, Men & Morals*, Harmondsworth: Penguin Books.

Gatens, M. (1991), *Feminism and Philosophy: Perspectives on Difference and Equality*, Indianapolis: Indiana University Press.

Gay, P. (1993), *The Cultivation of Hatred: The Bourgeois Experience, Victoria to Freud*, Volume 3, London: Harper Collins.

Germove, J. (1993), *Getting Away with Murder: Medical Negligence, Informed Consent and Access to Justice*, Department of Social Health Studies, University of Newcastle, New South Wales.

Gjertsen, D. (1989), *Science and Philosophy: Past and Present*, Harmondsworth: Penguin Books.

Gillespie, R. (1989), 'Research on Human Subjects: An Historical Overview', *Bioethics News*, January, pp. 4-15

Gilligan, C. (1993), *In a Different Voice: Psychological Theory and Women's Development*, Cambridge: Harvard University Press.

Goldstein, J. (1975), 'For Harold Lasswell: Some Reflections on Human Dignity, Entrapment, Informed Consent, and the Plea Bargain', *The Yale Law Journal*, vol. 84, pp. 683-703.

Grabosky P. and Sutton A. (eds), (1990), *Stains on a White Collar*, Sydney: The Federation Press.

Greschner, D. (1987), 'Judicial Approaches to Equality and Critical Legal Studies', in S. L. Martin and K. E. Mahoney, (eds), *Equality and Judicial Neutrality*, Toronto: Carswell, pp. 59-70.

Habermas, J. (1984), *The Theory of Communicative Action*, T. McCarthy (trans), Oxford: Polity Press.

Habermas, J. (1996), *Between Facts and Norms: Contributions to a Discourse Theory of Law and Democracy*, W. Rehg (trans), Cambridge: Polity Press.

Habermas, J. (1998), 'Paradigms of Law', in M. Rosenfeld and A. Arato (eds), *Habermas on Law and Democracy: Critical Exchanges*, Berkeley: University of California Press, pp. 13-25.

Harpwood, V. (1996), 'Medical Negligence: A Chink in the Armour of the Bolam Test?' [British] *Medico-Legal Journal*, vol. 64, Part 4, pp. 179-185.

Hart, H. L. A. (1958), 'Positivism and the Separation of Law and Morals', *Harvard Law Review*, vol. 71 (4), pp. 593-629.

Hart, H. L. A. (1961), *Concept of Law*, London: Clarendon Press.

Hart, H. L. A. (1963), *Law, Liberty and Morality*, London: Oxford University Press.

Harth, E. (1992), *Cartesian Women: Versions and Subversions of Rational Discourse in the Old Regime*, London: Cornell University Press.

Haug, M. and Lavin, B. (1983), *Consumerism in Medicine: Challenging Physician Authority*, Beverly Hills: Sage Publications

Hindress, B. (1996), *Discourses of Power: From Hobbes to Foucault*, Oxford: Blackwell.

Honneth, A. (1999), 'The Social Dynamics of Disrespect: Situating Critical Social Theory Today', in P. Dews (ed), *Habermas: A Critical Reader*, Oxford: Blackwell, pp. 320-337.

Hume, D. (1971), *A Treatise of Human Nature*, Oxford: Oxford University Press. First published 1740.

Illich, I. (1976), *Limits to Medicine*, Harmondsworth: Penguin Books.

Irigaray, L. (1993a), *An Ethics of Sexual Difference*, C. Burke and G. C. Gill (trans), New York: Cornell University Press.

Irigaray, L. (1993b), *Je, Tu, Nous: Toward a Culture of Difference*, A. Martin (trans), New York: Routledge.

Jones, J. H. (1981), *Bad Blood: The Tuskegee Syphilis Experiment*, New York: Free Press.

Kant, I. (1990), *Foundations of the Metaphysics of Morals and What is Enlightenment?* (2nd ed), Beck, L. W. (trans), New York: Macmillan. First published 1784, 1785.

Katz, J. (1977), 'Informed Consent – A Fairy Tale? Law's Vision', *University of Pittsburgh Law Review*, vol. 39 (2), pp. 137-174.

Katz, J. (1984), *The Silent World of Doctor and Patient*, New York: The Free Press.

Katz, J. (1992), 'The Consent Principle of the Nuremberg Code: Its Significance Then and Now', in G. J. Annas and M. A. Grodin (eds), *The Nazi Doctors and the Nuremberg Code: Human Rights in Human Experimentation*, New York: Oxford University Press, pp. 227-239.

Kelly, M. (1994), 'Foucault, Habermas, and the Self-Referentiality of Critique', in M. Kelly (ed), *Critique and Power: Recasting the Foucault/Habermas Debate*, Cambridge, Mass., and London: MIT Press, pp. 365-400.

Kennedy, D. (1979), 'The Structure of Blackstone's Commentaries', *Buffalo Law Review*, vol. 28, pp.209-382.

Kinley, D. (1998), 'The Legal Dimension of Human Rights', in D. Kinley, (ed), *Human Rights in Australian Law*, Sydney: The Federation Press, pp. 2-25.

Krugman, S. and Giles, J. P. (1976), 'Viral Hepatitis: New Light on an Old Disease', in S. Gorovitz, et al., (eds), *Moral Problems in Medicine*, Englewood Cliffs, New Jersey: Prentice-Hall, pp. 123-125.

Kumar, S. (1999), 'Doctors Still Involved in Cases of Torture Around the World', *The Lancet*, vol. 354, p. 1188.

Lacey, N. (1998), *Unspeakable Subjects: Feminist Essays in Legal and Social Theory*, Oxford: Hart Publishing.

Langer, E. (1976), 'Human Experimentation: New York Verdict Affirms Patient's Rights', in S. Gorovitz, et al., (eds), *Moral Problems in Medicine*, Englewood Cliffs, New Jersey: Prentice-Hall, pp. 142-150.

Larned, D. (1977), 'The Epidemic in Unnecessary Hysterectomy', in C. Dreifus (ed), *Seizing our Bodies: The Politics of Women's Health*, New York: Vintage Books, pp. 195-208.

Lavis, J. and Sullivan, T. (1999), 'Governing Health', in D. Drache and T. Sullivan, (eds), *Market Limits in Health Reform: Public Success, Private Failure*, London and New York: Routledge, pp. 312-328.

Law Reform Commission of Victoria, (1989), *Informed Decisions about Medical Procedures: Doctor and Patient Studies*, Canberra: Australian Government Publishing Service.

Law Reform Commission of Victoria, Australian Law Reform Commission, New South Wales Law Reform Commission, (1989), *Informed Decisions About Medical Procedures*, Canberra: Australian Government Publishing Service.

Lawrence, J. (1991), 'Inquiries into Psychiatry: Chelmsford and Townsville', *Medical Journal of Australia*, vol. 155, pp. 652-654.

Llewelyn, J. (1995), *Emmanuel Levinas: The Genealogy of Ethics*, London: Routledge.

Lloyd, G. (1993), *The Man of Reason: 'Male' and 'Female' in Western Philosophy*, (2nd ed), London: Routledge.

Locke, J. (1960), *Two Treatises of Government*, Cambridge: Cambridge University Press. First published 1690.

MacIntyre, A. (1985), *After Virtue: A Study in Moral Theory*, (2nd ed), London: Duckworth.

MacKinnon, C. A. (1991a), 'Difference and Dominance: On Sex Discrimination', in K. T. Bartlett and R. Kennedy, (eds), *Feminist Legal Theory: Readings in Law and Gender*, Boulder: Westview Press, pp. 81-94.

MacKinnon, C. A. (1991b), 'Feminism, Marxism, Method and the State', in K. T. Bartlett and R. Kennedy, (eds), *Feminist Legal Theory: Readings in Law and Gender*, Boulder: Westview Press, pp. 181-200.

McLean, S. A. M. (ed), (1981), *Legal Issues in Medicine*, Aldershot: Gower.

McLean, S. A. M. (ed), (1995), *Law Reform and Medical Injury Litigation*, Aldershot: Dartmouth.

McLean, S. A. M. (1995), 'Whither Medical Injury Law?' in S. A. M. McLean (ed), *Law Reform and Medical Injury Litigation*, Aldershot: Dartmouth, pp. 1-4.

McLean, S. A. M. (1999), *Old Law, New Medicine: Medical Ethics and Human Rights*, London and New York: Rivers Oram Publishers.

McNay, L. (1992), *Foucault and Feminism: Power, Gender and the Self*, Cambridge: Polity Press.

McNeill, P. M. (1993), *The Ethics and Politics of Human Experimentation*, Cambridge, New York and Melbourne: Cambridge University Press.

Maitland, I. (1997), 'The Limits of Business Regulation', in T. L. Beauchamp and N E. Bowie, (eds), *Ethical Theory and Business*, (5th ed), New Jersey: Prentice-Hall, pp. 126-135.

Malcolm, D. (1994), 'The High Court and Informed Consent: The Bolam Principle Abandoned', *Tort Law Review*, July, pp. 81-98.

Marmor, T. (1999), 'The Rage for Reform: Sense and Nonsense in Health Policy', in D. Drache and T. Sullivan, (eds), *Market Limits in Health Reform: Public Success, Private Failure*, London and New York: Routledge, pp. 260-272.

Martin, S. L. and Mahoney, K. E. (1987), 'Preface', in S. L. Martin and K. E. Mahoney, (eds), *Equality and Judicial Neutrality*, Toronto, Calgary and Vancouver: Carswell, pp. iii-v.

Merquior, J. G. (1991), *Foucault*, London: Fontana Press.

Miles, R. (1989), *The Women's History of the World*, London: Paladin.

Mill, J. S. (1972), 'On Liberty', in H. B. Acton (ed), *John Stuart Mill: Utilitarianism, Liberty, Representative Government*, London: J. M. Dent & Sons, pp. 63-120. First published 1859.

Mitchell, B. (1970), *Law, Morality and Religion in a Secular Society*, London: Oxford University Press.

Moller Okin, S. (1979), *Women in Western Political Thought*, London: Virago.

Moller Okin, S. (1989), *Justice, Gender and the Family*, New York: Basic Books.

Montesquieu, (1952), *The Spirit of Laws*, T. Nugent (trans), Chicago, London and Toronto: Encyclopedia Britannica. First published 1748.

Moynihan, R. (1998), *Too Much Medicine*, Sydney: ABC Books.

Mustard, F. (1999), 'Health, Health Care and Social Cohesion', in D. Drache and T. Sullivan, (eds), *Market Limits in Health Reform: Public Success, Private Failure*, London and New York: Routledge, pp. 329-350.

Nagel, T. (1991), *Equality and Partiality*, New York: Oxford University Press.

Nietzsche, F. (1990), *Beyond Good and Evil*, R. J. Hollingdale (trans), London: Penguin Books.

Nozick, R. (1974), *Anarchy, State and Utopia*, Oxford: Blackwell.

O'Neill, N. and Handley, R. (1994), *Retreat from Injustice: Human Rights in Australian Law*, Leichhardt, New South Wales: The Federation Press.

O'Faolain, J. and Martines, L. (eds), (1979), *Not in God's Image: Women in History*, London: Virago.

O'Sullivan, J. (unpd), *The Professional versus the Material Risks Standards of Risk Disclosure: The Appropriate Standard for Australia*, Master of Laws Thesis (1988), Monash University, Melbourne.

Owen, D. G. (1995), 'Why Philosophy Matters to Tort Law', in D. G. Owen, (ed), *Philosophical Foundations of Tort Law*, Oxford: Clarendon Press, pp. 1-27.

Paine, T. (1984), *Rights of Man*, Harmondsworth: Penguin Books. First published 1791.

Plato, (1994), *Gorgias*, R. Waterfield (trans), Oxford: Oxford University Press.

Pellegrino, E. D. and Thomasma, D. C. (1988), *For the Patient's Good: The Restoration of Beneficence in Health Care*, New York: Oxford University Press.

Perley, S. Fluss, S. Bankowski, Z. and Simon, F. (1992), 'The Nuremberg Code: An International Overview', in G. J. Annas and M. A. Grodin (eds), *The Nazi Doctors and the Nuremberg Code: Human Rights in Human Experimentation*, New York: Oxford University Press, pp. 149-173.

Pringle, R. (1998), *Sex and Medicine: Gender, Power and Authority in the Medical Profession*, Cambridge: Cambridge University Press.

Proctor, R. N. (1992), 'Nazi Doctors, Racial Medicine, and Human Experimentation', in G. J. Annas and M. A. Grodin (eds), *The Nazi Doctors and the Nuremberg Code: Human Rights in Human Experimentation*, New York: Oxford University Press, pp. 17-31.

Pross, C. (1992), 'Nazi Doctors, German Medicine, and Historical Truth', in G. J. Annas and M. A. Grodin (eds), *The Nazi Doctors and the Nuremberg Code: Human Rights in Human Experimentation*, New York: Oxford University Press, pp. 32-52.

Rabinow, P. (ed), (1984), *The Foucault Reader*, New York: Pantheon Books.

Rawls, J. (1971), *A Theory of Justice*, Oxford: Oxford University Press.

Rawls, J. (1996), *Political Liberalism*, New York: Columbia University Press.

Rawls, J. (1999), *The Law of Peoples*, Cambridge, Mass: Harvard University Press.

Reiss, H. (ed), (1991), *Kant: Political Writings*, H. B. Nisbet (trans), (2nd ed), Cambridge: Cambridge University Press.

Rice, S. (1988), *Some Doctors Make You Sick*, North Ryde, New South Wales: Angus & Robertson.

Richardson, W. J. (1995), 'The Irresponsible Subject', in A. T. Peperzak, (ed), *Ethics as First Philosophy: The Significance of Emmanuel Levinas for Philosophy, Literature and Religion*, New York and London: Routledge, pp. 123-131.

Robertson, G. (1991), 'Informed Consent Ten Years Later: The Impact of Reibl v Hughes', *The Canadian Bar Review*, vol. 70 (3), pp. 423-447.

Rosenfeld, M. (1998), 'Can Rights, Democracy, and Justice be Reconciled Through Discourse Theory? Reflections on Habermas's Proceduralist Paradigm of Law', in M. Rosenfeld and A. Arato (eds), *Habermas on Law and Democracy: Critical Exchanges*, Berkeley: University of California Press, pp. 82-112.

Ross, W. D. (1930), *The Right and the Good*, London: Oxford University Press.

Rothman, D. (1991), *Strangers at the Bedside: A History of How Law and Bioethics Transformed Medical Decision-Making*, New York: Basic Books.

Rothman, K. J. and Michels, K. B. (1994), 'The Continuing Unethical Use of Placebo Controls', *New England Journal of Medicine*, August, pp. 394-398.

Rozovsky, L. and Rozovsky, F. (1990), *The Canadian Law of Consent to Treatment*, Toronto and Vancouver: Butterworths.

Samuels, A. (1999), 'The Doctor and the Lawyer: Medico-Legal Problems Today', [British] *Medico-Legal Journal*, vol. 67, Part 1, pp. 11-39.

Sandel, M. (1984), 'Justice and the Good', in M. Sandel (ed), *Liberalism and its Critics*, Oxford: Blackwell.

Schaeffer, D. (1979), *Justice or Tyranny? A Critique of John Rawls's Theory of Justice*, London: Kennicat Press.

Schama, S. (1989), *Citizens: A Chronicle of the French Revolution*, London: Penguin Books.

Scheuerman, W. E. (1999), 'Between Radicalism and Resignation: Democratic Theory in Habermas's Between Facts and Norms', in P. Dews (ed), *Habermas: A Critical Reader*, Oxford: Blackwell, pp. 153-177.

Schultz, M. (1995), 'From Informed Consent to Patient Choice: A New Protected Interest', *The Yale Law Journal*, vol. 95 (2), pp. 219-299.

Scutt, J. A. and Graham, D. (1984), *For Richer, For Poorer: Money, Marriage and Property Rights*, Melbourne: Penguin Books.

Scutt, J. A. (1990), *Women and the Law: Commentary and Materials*, North Ryde, New South Wales: Law Book Company.

Scutt, J. A. (1997), *The Incredible Woman: Power & Sexual Politics, Volume 1*, Melbourne: Artemis Publishing.

Seabourne, G. (1995), 'The Role of the Tort of Battery in Medical Law', *Anglo-American Law Review*, vol. 24, pp. 265-298.

Shaw, G. B. (1971), *The Doctor's Dilemma*, Harmondsworth: Penguin Books. First published 1906.

Sherwin, S. (1992), *No Longer Patient: Feminist Ethics and Health Care*, Philadelphia: Temple University Press.

Sherwin, S. (1996), 'Feminism and Bioethics', in S. M. Wolf (ed), *Feminism and Bioethics: Beyond Reproduction*, New York: Oxford University Press, pp. 48-56.

Shklar, J. N. (1964), *Legalism*, Cambridge, Mass: Harvard University Press.

Shklar, J. (1984), *Ordinary Vices*, Cambridge, Mass: Harvard University Press.

Shklar, J. (1990), *The Faces of Injustice*, New Haven: Yale University Press.

Siggins, I. (1996), 'Professional Codes: Some Historical Antecedents', in M. Coady and S. Bloch (eds), *Codes of Ethics and the Professions*, Melbourne: Melbourne University Press, pp. 55-71.

Simanowitz, A. (1995), 'Law Reform and Medical Negligence Litigation: The UK Position', in S. A. M. McLean, (ed), *Law Reform and Medical Injury Litigation*, Aldershot: Dartmouth, pp. 119-146.

Sinclair, A. (1996), 'Codes in the Workplace: Organisational versus Professional Codes', in M. Coady and S. Bloch (eds), *Codes of Ethics and the Professions*, Melbourne: Melbourne University Press, pp. 88-108.

Skene, L. (1993), 'The Standard of Care in Relation to a Medical Practitioner's Duty of Disclosure', *Torts Law Journal*, vol. 1, pp. 103-113.

Skene, L. and Millwood, S. (1997), '"Informed Consent" to Medical Procedures: The Current Law in Australia, Doctors' Knowledge of the Law and their Practices in Informing Patients', in L. Shotton (ed), *Health Care Law and Ethics*, Katoomba, New South Wales: Social Science Press.

Smart, C. (1989), *Feminism and the Power of Law*, London: Routledge.

Somerville, M. A. (1981), 'Structuring the Issues in Informed Consent', *McGill Law Journal*, vol. 26, pp. 740-808.

Starr, P. (1982), *The Social Transformation of American Medicine*, New York: Basic Books.

Tan, K. F. (1987), 'Failure of Medical Advice: Trespass or Negligence?' *Legal Studies*, vol. 7, pp. 149-168.

Temkin, O. (1995), *Hippocrates in a World of Pagans and Christians*, Baltimore: Johns Hopkins University Press.

The Nuremberg Code, (1946), in *Trials of War Criminals before the Nuremberg Military Tribunals under Control Council Law No. 10*, vol.

2, 1949, Washington, D.C: United States Government Printing Office, pp. 181-182.

Turner, B. S. with Samson, C. (1995), *Medical Power and Social Knowledge*, (2nd ed), London: Sage Publications.

Unger, R. M. (1976, c1975), *Knowledge and Politics*, New York: Free Press.

Unger, R. M. (1986), *The Critical Legal Studies Movement*, Cambridge, Mass: Harvard University Press.

Unger, R. M. (1996), *What Should Legal Analysis Become?* London: Verso.

Unger, R. M. (1997), *Politics: The Central Texts*, Zhiyuan Cui (ed), London and New York: Verso.

Unger, R. M. (1998), *Democracy Realized: The Progressive Alternative*, London and New York: Verso.

Veatch, R. M. (1991), *The Patient-Physician Relation: The Patient as Partner, Part 2*, Bloomington and Indianapolis: Indiana University Press.

Veatch, R. M. (1993), 'Benefit/Risk Assessment: What Patients Can Know that Scientists Cannot', *Drug Information Journal*, vol. 27, pp. 1021-1029.

Wadlington, W. (1995), 'Law Reform and Damages for Medical Injury in the United States', in S. A. M. McLean, (ed), *Law Reform and Medical Injury Litigation*, Aldershot: Dartmouth, pp. 89-118.

Walton, M. (1998), *The Trouble with Medicine: Preserving the Trust Between Patients and Doctors*, St Leonards, New South Wales: Allen & Unwin.

Wasserstrom, R. A. (ed), (1971), *Morality and the Law*, Belmont, California: Wadsworth.

Weber, E. (1995), 'The Notion of Persecution in Levinas's Otherwise than Being or Beyond Essence', in A. T. Peperzak, (ed), *Ethics as First Philosophy: The Significance of Emmanuel Levinas for Philosophy, Literature and Religion*, New York and London: Routledge, pp. 69-76.

Weiss, K. (1977), 'What Medical Students Learn about Women', in C. Dreifus (ed), *Seizing Our Bodies: The Politics of Women's Health*, New York: Vintage Books, pp. 212-222.

Werhane, P. H. (1995), 'Levinas's Ethics: A Normative Perspective without Metaethical Constraints', in A. T. Peperzak, (ed), *Ethics as First Philosophy: The Significance of Emmanuel Levinas for Philosophy, Literature and Religion*, New York and London: Routledge, pp. 59-67.

Wertheim, M. (1995), *Pythagoras' Trousers: God, Physics and the Gender Wars*, New York: Random House.

Wilson, P. R. Chappell, D. and Lincoln, R. (1986), 'Policing Physician Abuse in British Columbia: An Analysis of Current Policies', *Canadian Public Policy*, vol. 12 (1), pp. 236-244.

Wilson, R. and Harrison, B. (1997), 'Are we Committed to Improving the Safety of Health Care?' *Medical Journal of Australia*, vol. 166, pp. 452-453.

Wilson, R. Runciman, N. Gibberd, R. Harrison, B. Newby, L. and Hamilton, J. (1995), 'The Quality in Australian Health Care Study', *Medical Journal of Australia*, vol. 163, pp. 458-471.

Wolf, S. M. (1988), 'Conflict Between Doctor and Patient', *Law, Medicine and Health Care*, vol. I6 (3-4), pp. 197-203.

Wolf, S. M. (1996), 'Gender and Feminism in Bioethics', in S. M. Wolf (ed), *Feminism and Bioethics: Beyond Reproduction*, New York: Oxford University Press, pp. 3-43.

Yack, B. (ed), (1996), *Liberalism Without Illusions: Essays on Liberal Theory and the Political Vision of Judith N. Shklar*, Chicago: University of Chicago Press.

Index